first ypres 1914

the birth of trench warfare

DAVID LOMAS

first ypres 1914

the birth of trench warfare

Praeger Illustrated Military History Series

PRAEGER

Westport, Connecticut
London

Library of Congress Cataloging-in-Publication Data

Lomas, David, 1939–
    First Ypres 1914: the birth of trench warfare / David Lomas.
       p. cm – (Praeger illustrated military history, ISSN 1547-206X)
    Originally published: Oxford: Osprey, 1998.
    Includes bibliographical references and index.
    ISBN 0-275-98291-2 (alk. paper)
    1. Ypres, 1st battle of, Ieper, Belgium, 1914. 2. World War, 1914–1918 – Trench warfare.
    I. Title. II. Series.
    D542.Y6L66   2004
    940.4'21–dc22   2003063223

British Library Cataloguing in Publication Data is available.

First published in paperback in 1998 by Osprey Publishing Limited, Elms Court,
Chapel Way, Botley, Oxford OX2 9LP. All rights reserved.

Copyright © 2004 by Osprey Publishing Limited

Library of Congress Catalog Card Number: 2003063223
ISBN: 0-275-98291-2
ISSN: 1547-206X

Praeger Publishers, 88 Post Road West, Westport, CT 06881
An imprint of Greenwood Publishing Group, Inc.
www.praeger.com

Printed in China through World Print Ltd.

The paper used in this book complies with the Permanent Paper Standard issued
by the National Information Standards Organization (Z39.48-1984).

10 9 8 7 6 5 4 3 2 1

ILLUSTRATED BY: Ed Dovey

CONTENTS

Key to maps

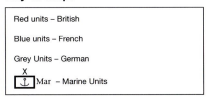

Red units – British

Blue units – French

Grey Units – German

Mar – Marine Units

Key to military series symbols

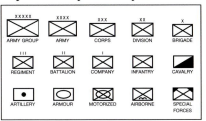

THE ROAD TO BATTLE

On 29 September 1914, Sir John French, the British commander in chief, wrote to Marshal Joffre, his French counterpart, stating that he wished 'to regain my original position on the left flank of the French Armies.'

The Great War was nearly two months old and the British Expeditionary Force had been in France for six weeks. It had fought at Mons and Le Cateau, retreated the long miles to Paris before the German advance was halted at the Marne, and finally supported the French offensive along the River Aisne.

For nearly three weeks, the British troops had stoically suffered a primitive and hazardous existence in waterlogged holes under constant shelling and small arms fire, interrupted by bouts of ferocious fighting. Seventy British infantry battalions, 15 cavalry regiments and 84 batteries of artillery grimly held 26 miles of front in miserable, soul-destroying conditions. The Marne and the Aisne had cost 18,000 casualties. In their six weeks of active service the BEF had lost over 36,000 men. There had been some reinforcements. The 4th Division, which had reached France in time to fight at Le Cateau, was now joined by the 6th Division to form III Corps. The BEF was still, however, a small force of just 163,897 all ranks.

Sir John's proposal was the result of hard thinking; the battle of the Aisne had degenerated into stalemate. It was thus an ideal moment to concentrate all British forces in one area. Other British troops were already landing and operating in the north – a hastily assembled force was at Antwerp – and more were on the way, among them the 7th Infantry Division and the Indian Corps.

The French Commander-in-Chief, Marshal Joffre, had a reputation for preserving an implacable calm, even under the most trying circumstances. His staff were under strict instructions never to disturb his night's rest and his meal times were similarly sacrosanct. Joffre's imperturbability did much to allay some of the more extravagant fears to which his British counterpart, Sir John French, was prone.

The BEF had stoically endured the primitive and muddy conditions of the Aisne battlefield, but there was a widespread feeling among officers and men that squatting in holes in churned-up mud was no way to fight a war. The move north to Flanders, where there was still a clear chance of fighting a war of movement was welcomed by everyone from the Commander-in-Chief down. These troops on the Aisne could equally well have been photographed in the Ypres salient a few weeks later.

It was logical that they should operate as one body. Further, supply lines would be much shorter close to the coast and the BEF could be reinforced quickly if necessary. Their presence would also bar the way to the Channel ports.

Sir John firmly believed that the BEF should not crouch in hastily-dug trenches under everlasting shell fire. It was an army trained for open warfare, and the flat plains of Flanders in the north still offered the chance to manoeuvre and fight a proper battle. Joffre, however, had reservations. He would have to find replacement troops to hold the muddy scrapes of trenches on the Aisne. The move would also divert precious railway wagons needed for sending French reinforcements to the north. Joffre still continued to suspect that Sir John would evacuate the BEF if things went badly and he regarded a location close to the Channel ports as a constant temptation for the British to retreat. He tactfully suggested that, although in broad agreement, the time was not quite right. The British commander disagreed and curtly informed Joffre that the first British troops would depart on 3 October.

Joffre accepted the inevitable. The timetable was agreed and the BEF went north. I Corps, the last to leave the battleground, reached Haze-brouck on 19 October.

THE OPPOSING COMMANDERS

THE GERMAN COMMANDERS

Erich von Falkenhayn, was Minister for War in August 1914; he succeeded von Moltke when the Schlieffen Plan failed but kept his ministerial post, which gave him immense power. Acutely perceptive, highly intelligent and ruthlessly determined, Falkenhayn was concerned with military ability, not the social standing of his subordinates. His lack of deference and decisive manner gave new urgency to the German High Command.

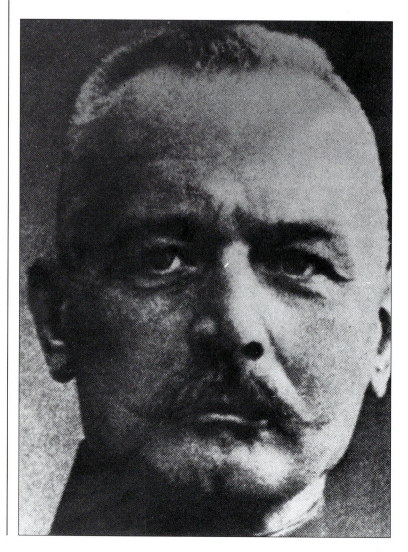

Erich von Falkenhayn, Chief of the German General Staff, was an immensely capable commander who demanded the utmost effort from his subordinates. A firm believer in swift and decisive action, he took little notice of excuses – officers who failed to deliver were quickly relieved of their responsibilities.

Crown Prince Rupprecht of Bavaria commanded the Sixth Army in 1914. Born in 1869, he had spent his working life as a soldier. He was resolute, not prone to panic, and had considerable common sense. Although his career was not uninfluenced by his royal blood, he was an effective army commander.

Grand Duke Albrecht of Württemburg's status definitely helped his career. It was freely alleged that he was promoted out of harm's way as quickly as possible. He commanded the Fourth Army, but it was generally assumed that it was effectively controlled by the Chief of Staff, Maj.Gen. Ilse.

Grand Duke Albrecht, commanding the German Fourth Army was not rated as a great commander by his contemporaries, his position owing more to his noble birth than innate ability.

THE ALLIED COMMANDERS

Field Marshal Sir John French, Commander-in-Chief of the British Expeditionary Force, went to France in 1914 with high hopes. Like very many others, he assumed that the war would be short and he was determined to win a share of glory from it. Irascible and prone to high blood pressure, he distrusted his French allies, despite having a holiday home in Normandy and a French son-in-law. Mercurial by temperament, he plunged from optimism to gloom in moments. He showed great skill in the South African War and was much admired as a fighting soldier. However, he bore grudges and imagined slights and insults where none were intended. He and Kitchener, the British Minister of War, distrusted each other. French further sensed a conspiracy on finding that three of his four Corps commanders had served under Kitchener in the Sudan. This was no recipe for a useful relationship.

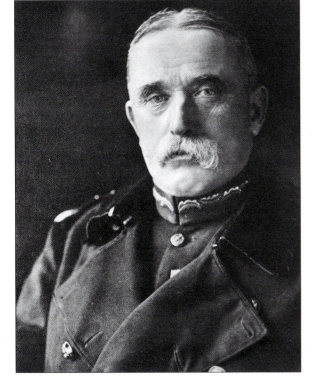

Ferdinand Foch commanded the French Armies in the North; as such, he liaised closely with Sir John French and his supreme optimism was of great help when dealing with the temperamental British commander. Foch had great personal courage and believed passionately that the only hope of victory was in consistently attacking the enemy. His experiences in the first weeks of the war had, however, moderated his enthusiasm for unbridled offensives as he learned the difficulties of operating with tired and frightened troops. He was, therefore, always ready to adopt a defensive position, but never failed to insist that the enemy also felt terror and fatigue and could succumb to attack.

Sir John French, the Commander-in-Chief of the BEF, was personally brave and enjoyed a great rapport with his men. He was, though, subject to great swings of mood, bounding from enthusiastic optimism to utter gloom in a very short period of time. Many of his contemporaries found it difficult to work with him as French was inclined to see insults and slights where none existed, and his reaction was often choleric. The sheer scale of the war was soon to exceed anything that he, in common with many other commanders and politicians, had ever contemplated.

THE OPPOSING ARMIES

THE GERMAN ARMY

Like the other combatants, Germany needed more fighting men. Reinforcements for the field armies of August 1914 were available for about 60 per cent of the private soldiers but only a quarter of the highly trained officers and NCOs could be replaced. To do more would strip the training camps of instructors and hamper the flow of new recruits.

As War Minister, Falkenhayn had authorised the formation of new divisions shortly after the war began. They were recruited from the many young men who had not been conscripted during peacetime, and were supplemented with older soldiers from the reserve *Landwehr* and *Landsturm*. Recalled regular officers became regimental and battalion commanders. Platoons were commanded by cadets awaiting com-

Falkenhayn's aim of capturing Calais included a plan to force a passage along the coast, taking the Channel ports one by one. This photograph, which clearly shows a bowler-hatted civilian (bottom centre) strolling with complete unconcern among the soldiers, was taken after the fall of Antwerp as the Germans prepared to advance on Ostend.

missions or specially chosen NCOs. The NCO strength of the new divisions was found among the *Landsturm* or *Landwehr*. Enthusiastic, eager to fight, totally untrained, they were still valuable manpower and provided six new Army Corps. Four of these, the XXII, XXIII, XXVI and XXVII Reserve Corps were earmarked for the Flanders offensive and became the German Fourth Army.

Other troops were withdrawn from France; VII, XIII, XIV and XIX Corps formed a new Sixth Army under Crown Prince Rupprecht. This itself would later be reinforced by untrained volunteers from Bavaria. There was a further source of men – the cavalry could be stripped of their horses and fight as infantry. The days of glittering lances and fluttering pennons were all but over.

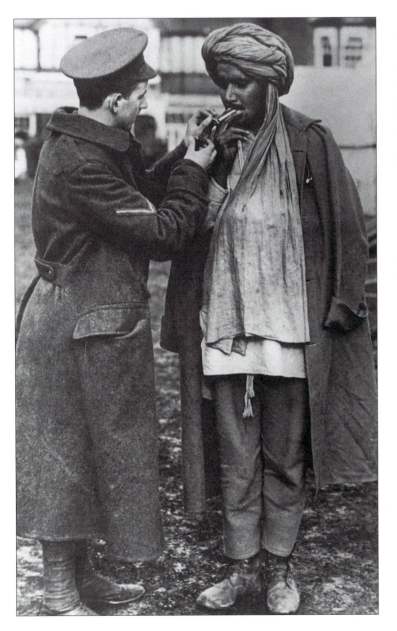

THE BRITISH ARMY

The British Army of 1914 was a long-service volunteer force which had reached a very high professional standard. The original BEF needed a large proportion of Reservists to bring it up to war strength in August 1914 and reinforcements were dwindling. They could be found from the Territorial Army, the 'Saturday Night Soldiers', who were embodied on the outbreak of war, although Kitchener considered them of little use. The need for reinforcements, though, was vital and the time was fast approaching when the Territorials would go to war.

In the meantime, an Indian Army Corps was on its way to supplement the BEF. There was one further and priceless addition: units from the overseas garrisons of the Empire, which needed very few Reservists to complete their War Establishment, were formed into the 7th Infantry and 3rd Cavalry Divisions in England. Their average length of service was five years and they were at the peak of their efficiency as fighting soldiers.

'Comrades In Arms – "Tommy" supplies a light to one of our wounded gallant Indian soldiers.' The arrival of Indian troops in France enabled the popular press of the day to explode in paroxysms of Imperial jingoist prose, and the original caption to this picture is restrained in comparison to some others – the phrase 'dusky warriors' was much in favour. The contribution of the Indian Army in 1914 was invaluable and their gallantry is often overlooked.

THE FRENCH ARMY

The French Army suffered severely in the first two months of the war, losing more than 250,000 men in August alone. The Aisne fighting further cut their numbers. Nonetheless, the French soldier was fiercely determined to repel the Germans and fought with great courage and tenacity. The French had always conscripted a high proportion of the male population and there was no large pool of volunteer replacements available. Like the British, however, they were able to draw on overseas garrisons and colonial troops and much rested with the French Territorials. These were not, as in Britain, volunteers. They were men in the last 14 years of their 25 year active and reserve obligation with a sprinkling of others unfit for full service. Seemingly lacking in martial ardour, often shabby in appearance, comfortable rather than disciplined, they made a vital contribution to the Allied success.

The French cavalry emulated the Germans and the British and manned the primitive trenches. There was no place for glorious cavalry charges in the new warfare.

First Ypres has generally been regarded by the British as a battle fought by the BEF alone against the Germans. In truth, the French and Belgian Armies were equally involved – Foch himself acidly observed in his Memoirs that 'On October 31st the French held about 15 miles of front, the British 12. On November 5th, the French held 18 miles and the British 9. It can be seen that the French troops, both as to length of front occupied and numbers engaged, had to sustain the major part of the battle. It would therefore be contrary to the truth to speak of the battle and victory of Ypres as exclusively British.' Foch excluded the British front to the south of Ypres from this analysis, but there is no argument that First Ypres was not an exclusively private contest between British and Germans. In this photograph, French cycle troops are shown going to Ypres.

THE BELGIAN ARMY

The Belgian field army – six infantry and one cavalry division – had spent most of the war so far retreating from superior numbers of German troops. Their equipment was poor and their morale had suffered, but they fought gallantly along the Meuse and held their positions on the left of the Allies despite strenuous enemy efforts to dislodge them. After the fall of Antwerp, the Belgians established a defensive line from Nieuport to Dixmude. They would hold it throughout the war.

All of the armies were short of supplies. Replenishment was a problem, for the scale of the fighting was already beyond what anyone had imagined possible. The German Army was short of heavy calibre ammunition and other equipment. Falkenhayn inaugurated a policy of *notbehelf* – makeshift or stopgap. The dead and wounded could yield arms, ammunition and equipment; food could be taken from the occupied territory. Rations for German soldiers took precedence over food for conquered civilians.

The French were in particular need of artillery ammunition. Their 75mm quick-firers were using 50,000 rounds every single day and French industry produced less than half of that. Units were instructed to return all cartridge cases to help speed production. Garrisons in less immediate danger were ransacked for supplies for use by units closer to the enemy. It was another instance of crisis management or more trenchantly, *pis-aller* – makeshift or stopgap.

The British Army were short of nearly everything. It had been starved of funds in peacetime in preference to spending on the Royal Navy. The BEF improvised where it could and went without when it couldn't. For every army, the story was the same, *notbehelf, pis-aller*, makeshift. It was, as one old soldier remembered, 'enough to make the brightest weep.'

Alongside the concept of 'gallant little Belgium' in the British popular press, was the esoteric problem of convincing animal lovers in England that the dog-pulled machine gun trolley of the Belgian army involved no cruelty. A number of writers took extravagant steps to assure British readers that the dogs were well treated and the captions to photographs like this one reinforced the message that the dogs positively enjoyed the work.

ORDER OF BATTLE

THE BEF

Commander-in-Chief: Gen. Sir John French

I CORPS

Lt.Gen. Sir Douglas Haig

1st DIVISION

Maj. Gen. S. Lomax

1ST (GUARDS) BRIGADE
    1st Coldstream Guards
    1st Scots Guards
    1st Black Watch
    1st Camerons
    London Scottish

2ND BRIGADE
    2nd Royal Sussex
    1st Loyal North Lancs.
    1st Northern
    2nd KRRC

3RD BRIGADE
    1st Queen's
    1st South Wales Borders
    1st Gloster
    2nd Welch

MOUNTED TROOPS
    A Squad. 15th Hussars
    1st Cyclist Coy.

ARTILLERY
    XXV Bde. RFA
    XXVI Bde. RFA
    XXXIX Bde. RFA
    XLIII (How.)Bde. RFA
    26th Heavy Bty.

ENGINEERS
    23rd & 26th Field Coys. RE

2nd DIVISION

Maj.Gen. C.Monro

4TH (GUARDS) BRIGADE
    2nd Grenadier Guards
    2nd & 3rd Coldstream Guards
    1st Irish Guards
    1st Hertfordshire

5TH BRIGADE
    2nd Worcestershire
    2nd Ox & Bucks LI
    2nd Highland LI
    2nd Connaught Rangers

6TH BRIGADE
    1st King's
    2nd South Stafford
    1st Royal Berkshire
    1st KRRC

MOUNTED TROOPS
    B Squad. 15th Hussars,
    2nd Cyclist Coy.

ARTILLERY
    XXXIV Bde. RFA
    XXXVI Bde. RFA
    XLI Bde. RFA
    XLIV (How.) Bde. RFA
    35th Heavy Bty.

ENGINEERS
    5th & IIth Field Coys.

II CORPS

Gen. Sir H. Smith-Dorrien

3rd DIVISION

Maj.Gen. H. Hamilton

7TH BRIGADE
    3rd Worcestershire
    2nd South Lancashire
    1st Wiltshire
    2nd Royal Irish Rifles

8TH BRIGADE
    2nd Royal Scots
    2nd Royal Irish
    4th Middlesex
    1st Devonshire
    1st Honourable Artillery Company

9TH BRIGADE
    1st Northumberland Fusiliers
    4th Royal Fusiliers
    1st Lincolns
    1st Royal Scots Fusiliers

MOUNTED TROOPS
    C Squad. 15th Hussars
    3rd Cyclist Coy.

ARTILLERY
    XXIII Bde. RFA
    XL Bde. RFA
    XLII Bde. RFA
    XXX (How.) Bde. RFA
    48th Heavy Bty.

ENGINEERS
    56th & 57th Field Coys. RE

5th DIVISION

Maj.Gen. Sir C. Fergusson

13TH BRIGADE
    2nd KOSB
    2nd DWR
    1st RWK
    2nd KOYLI

14TH BRIGADE
    2nd Suffolk,
    1st East Surrey
    1st DCLI
    2nd Manchester

Sir Douglas Haig commanded I Corps of the BEF. Haig believed emphatically in careful and thorough planning and his staff was probably the best in the Army. He took particular care to establish and maintain excellent relationships with his French counterparts, a policy that paid off handsomely during the desperate fighting at First Ypres. Never a man to court popularity, he nonetheless earned a high reputation from the men of I Corps for his uncompromising attention to detail.

Sir Horace Smith-Dorrien, commanding II Corps, was a determined soldier of considerable ability. A fighting soldier with a minimum of staff experience, 'Our "Orace"' was greatly admired by his soldiers. Unlike Haig and Joffre, who both maintained an exterior calm under the most trying conditions, Smith-Dorrien's temper was usually on a short fuse and he could explode in violent rage with apparently little provocation.

Sir William Pulteney, the commander of III Corps and can hardly be described as a thrusting or vigorous leader. He found it difficult to delegate decision-making, a trait which inhibited his brigade and divisional commanders who thus tended to refer quite minor matters to him. This, allied with a natural caution, led to missed opportunities although, in retrospect, it can be argued that Pulteney's reluctance to charge ahead actually proved to be a wise course.

In theory, communication on the battlefield was a well-controlled affair. Signalling by flag, heliograph and by wireless was diligently practised simply because there was little alternative. This picture shows signallers using semaphore with an admirable neatness. A soldier with a telescope, another with a notepad and the two windswept officers give a misleading picture of how easy it would be. As it was, communications collapsed in many actions throughout the war, leaving the commanders virtually powerless.

15TH BRIGADE
  1st Norfolk
  1st Bedfordshire
  1st Cheshire
  1st Dorset

MOUNTED TROOPS
  A Squad. 19th Hussars
  5th Cyclist Coy.

ARTILLERY
  XV Bde. RFA
  XXVII Bde. RFA
  XXVIII Bde. RFA
  VIII (How.) Bde. RFA
  108th Heavy Bty.

ENGINEERS
  17th & 59th Field Coys. RE

III CORPS

Maj. Gen. W. Pulteney

4th DIVISION

Maj.Gen. H. Wilson

10TH BRIGADE
  1st Royal Warwick
  2nd Seaforths
  1st Royal Irish Fusilier
  2nd Royal Dublin Fusiliers

11 BRIGADE
  1st Somerset LI
  1st East Lancs
  1st Hampshires
  1st Rifle Bde

12TH BRIGADE
  1st King's Own
  2nd Lancs Fusiliers
  2nd Inniskilling Fusiliers
  2nd Essex

MOUNTED TROOPS
  B Squad. 19th Hussars
  4 Cyclist Coy.

ARTILLERY
  XIV Bde. RFA
  XXIX Bde. RFA
  XXXII Bde. RFA
  XXXVII (How.) Bde. RFA
  31 Heavy Bty.

ENGINEERS
  7 & 9 Field Coys. RE

6th DIVISION

Maj.Gen. J.L. Keir

16TH BRIGADE
  1stThe Buffs
  1st Leicester
  1st KSLI
  2nd Yorks & Lancs.

17TH BRIGADE
  1st Royal Fusiliers
  1st North Stafford
  2nd Leinster
  3rd Rifle Bde.

18TH BRIGADE
  1st West Yorks.
  1st East Yorks.
  2nd Foresters
  2nd Durhams LI.

MOUNTED TROOPS
  C Squad. 19th Hussars
  6th Cyclist Coy.

19TH BDE.
  2nd Royal Welch Fusiliers
  2nd Cameronians
  1st Middlesex
  2nd Argyll & Sutherland Highlanders

ARTILLERY
  II Bde. RFA
  XXIV Bde. RFA
  XXXVIII Bde. RFA
  XII (How.) Bde. RFA
  24th Heavy BTY RGA.

ENGINEERS
  12th& 38th Field Coys. RE

ROYAL FLYING CORPS

Brig.Gen. Sir D. Henderson
  HQ Wireless unit
  2nd, 3rd, 4th, 5th, & 6th Aeroplane
  Squadrons (63 machines)

CAVALRY CORPS

Lt.Gen. E.H.H. Allenby

1st CAVALRY DIVISION

Maj.Gen. H. de Lisle

1ST CAVALRY BRIGADE
  2nd Dragoon Guards
  5th Dragoon Guards
  11th Hussars
  1st Signal Troop

2ND CAVALRY BRIGADE
  4th Dragoon Guards;
  9th Lancers
  18th Hussars;
  2nd Signal Troop

CAVALRY DIVISIONAL TROOPS

Artillery	VII Bde. RHA
Engineers	1st Field Squad. RE
Signal Services	1st Signal Squad.
ASC	1st Cav. Div. Supply Column
Medical Units	1st & 3rd Cav.
	Field Ambulances

IV CORPS

Lt. Gen. Sir H. Rawlinson

2nd CAVALRY DIVISION

Maj.Gen. H. Gough

3RD CAVALRY BRIGADE
- 4th Hussars
- 5th Lancers
- 16th Lancers
- 3rd Signal Troop

4TH CAVALRY BRIGADE
- Composite Regt. of Household Cavalry
- 6th Dragoon Guards
- 3rd Hussars
- 4th Signal Troop

5TH CAVALRY BRIGADE
- 2nd Dragoons
- 12th Lancers
- 20th Hussars
- 5th Signal Troop

CAVALRY DIVISIONAL TROOPS:

Artillery	II Bde. RHA
Engineers	2nd Field Squad. RE
Signal Services	2nd Signal Squad.
ASC	2nd Cav. Div. Supply Column
Medical Units	2nd, 4th & 5th Cav. Field Ambulances

7TH DIVISION

Maj.Gen. T. Capper

20TH BRIGADE
- 1st Grenadier Guards
- 2nd Scots Guards
- 2nd Border
- 2nd Gordan Highlanders

21ST BRIGADE
- 2nd Bedfordshire
- 2nd Green Howards
- 2nd Royal Scots Fusiliers
- 2nd Wiltshire

22ND BRIGADE
- 2nd Queen's
- 2nd Royal Warwickshire
- 1st Royal Welch Fusiliers
- 1st South Staffordshire

DIVISIONAL TROOPS:

Mounted troops	Northumberland Hussars
	7th Cyclist Coy.
Artillery	XIV Bde. RHA
	XXII Bde. RFA
	XXXV Bde. RFA
	III(Heavy)Bde. RGA
	7th Div. Ammunition Column
Engineers RE	54th & 55th Field Coys.
Signals	7th Signal Coy.
ASC	7th Div. Train
Medical Units	21st, 22nd & 23rd Field Ambulances

3RD CAVALRY DIVISION

Maj.Gen. J. Byng

6TH CAVALRY BRIGADE
- 3rd Dragoon Guards
- 1st Royal Dragoons
- 10th Hussars

7TH CAVALRY BRIGADE
- 1st and 2nd Life Guards
- Royal Horse Guards

CAVALRY DIVISIONAL TROOPS:

Artillery	XV Bde. RHA
Engineers	3rd Field Squad. RE
Signals	3rd Signal Squad.
ASC	33rd Cav. Div. Supply Column
Medical Units	6th & 7th Cav. Field Ambulances

The Defence of Antwerp was considered a vital feature of Allied strategy by many pundits. Sir John French had proposed sending troops there at the outbreak of war and it was thought that a strong force in Antwerp would be able to strike the Germans in the flank and stop their advance. Churchill sent a hastily-raised Royal Naval Division of reservists and new recruits to help defend Antwerp. This photograph shows them 'manning well-constructed trenches' on the outskirts of the city, a principal feature of which appears to be the wooden crates at the back upon which to hang greatcoats!

INDIAN CORPS

Lt.Gen. Sir J. Willcocks

THE LAHORE DIVISION

Lt.Gen. H. Watkis

FEROZEPORE BRIGADE
1st Connaught Rangers
9th Bhopal Inf.
57th Wilde's Rifles
129th Duke of Connaught's Own Baluchis

JULLUNDER BRIGADE
1st Manchester
15th Ludhiana Sikhs
47th Sikhs
59th Scinde Rifles

THE MEERUT DIVISION

Lt.Gen. C. Anderson

DEHRA DUN BRIGADE
1st Seaforth Highlanders
6th Jat L.I.
2/22nd King Edward's Own Gurkha Rifles,
1/9th Gurkha Rifles

GARWAT BRIGADE
2nd Leicester Regt.
1/39th Garhwal Rifles
2/39th Garhwal Rifles
2/3rd Queen Alexandra's Own Gurkha Rifles

BAREILLY BRIGADE
2nd Black Watch
41st Dogras
58th Vaughan's Rifles
2/8th Gurkha Rifles

DIVISIONAL TROOPS:
Mounted Troops	4th Cav.
Artillery	IV Bde. RFA
	IX Bde. RFA
	XIII Bde. RFA
	110th Heavy Battery RGA
	Meerut Divisional Ammunition Column
Engineers	1st King George's Own Sappers & Miners (3rd and 4th Coys.)
Signals	Meerut Signal Coy.
Pioneers	107th Pioneers
S&T	Meerut Div. Train
Medical Units	19th & 20th British Field Ambulance
	128th, 129th & 130th Indian Field Ambulance

UNITS AT ANTWERP

ROYAL NAVAL DIVISION:

Maj.Gen. A. Paris

ROYAL MARINE BRIGADE
Chatham Bn. RMLI
Portsmouth Bn.
Plymouth Bn.
Deal Bn.

1ST ROYAL NAVAL BDE
1st (Drake) Bn.
2nd (Hawke) Bn.
3rd (Benbow) Bn.
4th (Collingwood) Bn.

2ND ROYAL NAVAL BDE
5th (Nelson)Bn.
6th (Howe) Bn.
7th (Hood) Bn.
8th (Anson) Bn.

THE FRENCH VIII ARMY

Commander: Gen. D'Urbal

IX CORPS

Gen. Dubois

17th DIVISION

Gen. Guignabaudet

33RD BRIGADE	Gen. Moussy
34TH BRIGADE	Gen. Briant
304TH BRIGADE	Gen. Dumay

18th DIVISION

Gen. Lefevre

35TH BRIGADE	Gen. Kopp
36TH BRIGADE	Gen. Lestoquois

6th CAVALRY DIVISION

Gen. Requichot

5TH CUIRASSIER BRIGADE	Col. Bertoli
6TH DRAGOON BRIGADE	Gen Laperrine
6TH LIGHT BRIGADE	Gen. Morel

7th CAVALRY DIVISION

Gen. Hely d'Oissel

6TH CUIRASSIER BRIGADE	Gen. Taufflieb
1ST DRAGOON BRIGADE	Col. Zeude
7TH LIGHT BRIGADE	Gen. de Bersaucourt

XVI CORPS

Gen. Grossetti

32nd DIVISION

Gen. Bouchez

63RD BRIGADE	Col. de Woillemont
64TH BRIGADE	Col. Magnan

43rd DIVISION

Gen. Lanquetot

85TH BRIGADE	Gen. Guillemat
86TH BRIGADE	Gen. Olleris

39th DIVISION

Gen. Danant

77TH BRIGADE	Gen. Wirbel
78TH BRIGADE	Gen. Gérome

31st DIVISION

Gen. Vidal

61ST BRIGADE	Gen. Bernard
62ND BRIGADE	Gen. Xardel

XXXII CORPS

Gen. Humbert

38th DIVISION

Gen. Muteau

75TH BRIGADE	Col. Vuillemin
76TH BRIGADE	Col. Vallet

42nd DIVISION

Gen. Duchesne

83RD BRIGADE	Col. Claudon
84TH BRIGADE	Col. Deville

89th TERRITORIAL DIVISION

Gen. Boucher

177TH BRIGADE	Col. Vandenberg
178TH BRIGADE	Col. de Percy

4th CAV. DIVISION

Gen de Buyer

3RD CUIRASSIER BRIGADE   Gen. de Monpoly
4TH DRAGOON BRIGADE   Gen. Dodelier
4TH LIGHT BRIGADE   Gen. de Boissieu
MARINE FUSILIER BRIGADE   Admiral Ronac'h

XX CORPS

Gen. Balfourier

11th DIVISION

Gen. Ferry

21ST BRIGADE   Col.Aimé
22ND BRIGADE   Gen. de Lobit

(39TH DIVISION LENT TO XVI CORPS)

26th DIVISION

Gen. Hallouin

51ST BRIGADE   Gen. Delaporte
52ND BRIGADE   Col. Dubois

II CAVALRY CORPS

Gen. de Mitry

87th TERRITORIAL DIVISION

Gen. Roy

173RD BRIGADE   Col. Conte
174TH BRIGADE   Gen. Couillaud

5th CAV. DIVISION

Gen. Allenou

3RD DRAGOON BRIGADE   Col. Robillot
7TH DRAGOON BRIGADE   Col. Hennocque
5TH LIGHT BRIGADE   Gen. de Cornulier Lucinière

9th CAV. DIVISION

Gen. de L'Espée

1ST CUIRASSIER BRIGADE   Gen. Gendron
9TH DRAGOON BRIGADE   Gen. de Sailly
16TH DRAGOON BRIGADE   Gen. de Sereville

I CAVALRY CORPS

Gen. Conneau

1st CAVALRY DIVISION

Gen. Mazel

2ND CUIRASSIER BRIGADE   Gen. Louvat
5TH DRAGOON BRIGADE   Col. Feraud
11TH DRAGOON BRIGADE   Gen. Corvisart

3rd CAVALRY DIVISION

Gen. de Lastours

4TH CUIRASSIERS BRIGADE   Col. Gouzil
13TH DRAGOON BRIGADE   Gen. Leorat
3RD LIGHT BRIGADE   Gen. de Villestreux

10th CAVALRY DIVISION

Gen. de Contades

10TH DRAGOON BRIGADE   Gen Champvallier
15TH DRAGOON BRIGADE   Gen. Grellet

French colonial troops on the way to Ypres. Like Britain, France did not hesitate to call on the soldiers of her overseas territories. As with the Indian troops, the French North African soldiers suffered badly in the cold and wet conditions of Flanders. Their uniforms, designed for service in hot climates, were of little use in Europe. An interesting footnote is that Haig, on his own initiative, supplied 10,000 rations of bully beef to the Moroccans under the command of Gen. de Maud'huy when he learned that they were short of food. Their enthusiastic reception of the gift would have astonished the BEF who were becoming heartily sick of it as a daily diet. De Maud'huy's thanks were eloquent – 'Nothing could touch me more deeply,' he wrote, 'than your kindness towards my half-starved soldiers, and those 10,000 rations are a gift I shall always remember.'

THE GERMAN ARMY

FOURTH ARMY

Commander: General Duke Albert of Württemburg
Chief of Staff: Maj.Gen. Ilse

III RESERVE CORPS

Gen. von Beseler

5th RESERVE DIV.

9TH RESERVE BRIGADE
4th & 48th Reserve Regts.

10TH RESERVE BRIGADE
12th & 52nd Reserve Regts.

6th RESERVE DIV.

11TH RESERVE BRIGADE
25th & 35th Reserve Regts.

12TH RESERVE BRIGADE
24th & 26th Reserve Regts.

4th ERSATZ DIVISION

9TH ERSATZ BRIGADE
9th, 10th, 11th, 12th Brandenburg Ersatz Bns.

13TH ERSATZ BRIGADE
13th, 14th, 15th, 16th Brandenburg Ersatz Bns.

33RD ERSATZ BRIGADE
34th, 35th, 36th, 81st Brandenburg Ersatz Bns.

XXII RESERVE CORPS

Gen. von Falkenhayn

43rd RESERVE DIV.

201st, 202nd, 203rd, 204th Reserve Regts.
15th Reserve Jaeger Bn.

44TH RESERVE DIV.

205th, 206th, 207th, 208th Reserve Regts.
16th Reserve Jaeger Bn.

XXIII RESERVE CORPS

Gen. von Kleist

45TH RESERVE DIV.

209th, 210th, 211th, 212th Reserve Regts.
17th Jaeger Bn.

46TH RESERVE DIV.

213th, 214th, 215th, 216th Reserve Regts.
18th Reserve Jaeger Bn.

XXVI RESERVE CORPS

Gen. von Hügel

51st RESERVE DIV.

233rd, 234th, 235th, 236th Reserve Regts.
23rd Reserve Jaeger Bn.

52nd RESERVE DIV.

237th, 238th, 239th, 245th Reserve Regts.
24th Reserve Jaeger Bn.

XXVII RESERVE CORPS

Lt.Gen. von Carlowitz
(27 Oct. Gen. von Schubert)

53rd RESERVE DIV. (SAXON)

241st, 242nd, 243rd, 244th Reserve Regts.
25th Reserve Jaeger Bn.

54th RESERVE DIV. (WÜRTTEMBURG)

245th, 246th, 247th, 248th Reserve Regts.
26th Reserve Jaeger Bn.

Attached at various times:

9TH RESERVE DIVISION

17TH RESERVE BRIGADE
7th & 19th Reserve Regts.

This quite remarkable photograph, which was undoubtedly taken in a Flemish town in 1914, claims to show a barricade manned by Belgian troops under attack from a German armoured car during the retreat from Antwerp towards the French border. Unlike many photographs of the time, this one communicates a definite urgency and is probably one of the few pictures of the period actually taken in action.

18TH RESERVE BRIGADE,
  6th & 47th Reserve Regts.
  5th Reserve Jäger Bn.

6TH BAVARIAN RESERVE DIVISION

(SEE XIV RESERVE CORPS)

MARINE DIVISION

1ST MARINE BRIGADE
1ST MATROSEN & 1ST MARINE BRIGADE
2ND MARINE BRIGADE
2ND MATROSEN & 2ND MARINE BRIGADE
37TH LANDWEHR BRIGADE
  73rd & 74th Landwehr Regts.38th
LANDWEHR BRIGADE
  77th & 78th Landwehr Regts.
2ND ERSATZ BRIGADE
  1st & 2nd Ersatz Regts.

SIXTH ARMY

Commander: Crown Prince Ruprecht of Bavaria
Chief of Staff: Maj.Gen. von Delmensingen

II CORPS

Gen. von Linsingen

3RD DIVISION

5TH BRIGADE
  2nd & 9th Grenadier Regts.
6TH BRIGADE
  4th Fusilier & 42nd Regts.

4TH DIVISION

7TH BRIGADE
  4th & 149th Regts.
8TH BRIGADE
  49th & 140th Regts.

VII CORPS

Gen. von Claer

13TH DIVISION

25TH BRIGADE
  13th & 158th Regts.
26TH BRIGADE
  15th & 55th Regts.

14TH DIVISION

27TH BRIGADE
  16th & 53rd Regts.
79TH BRIGADE
  56th & 57th Regts.

XIII CORPS

Gen. von Fabeck

26TH DIVISION

51ST BRIGADE
  119th Grenadier & 125th Regts.
52ND BRIGADE
  121st & 122nd Fusilier Regts.

Crown Prince Rupprecht of Bavaria, commander of the Sixth Army, was in the opinion of some people, the rightful heir to the British throne because of his descent from the Stuart line. He was a competent commander whose war memoirs make most interesting reading.

German troops assemble in Brussels. Many of the soldiers here were to be sent against the BEF.

25TH RESERVE DIV.

49TH RESERVE BRIGADE
116th & 118th Reserve Regts.
50TH RESERVE BRIGADE
83rd Reserve & 168th Regts.

XIX (SAXON) CORPS

Gen. von Laffert

24TH DIVISION

47TH BRIGADE
139th & 179th Regts.
48TH INF. BRIGADE
106th & 107th Regts.

40TH DIVISION

88TH BRIGADE
10th & 181st Regts.
89TH BRIGADE
133rd & 134th Regts.

XIV RESERVE CORPS

Gen. von Loden

26TH RESERVE DIV.

51ST RESERVE BRIGADE
180th Regt. & 119th & 99th Reserve Regts.
52ND RESERVE BRIGADE
120th & 121st Reserve Regts.

6TH BAVARIAN RESERVE DIVISION

12TH BAVARIAN RESERVE BRIGADE
16th & 17th Bavarian Reserve Regts.
14TH BAVARIAN RESERVE BRIGADE
20th, 21st, & 9th Bavarian Reserve Regts.

ARMY GROUP FABECK

(27 Oct – 20 Nov 1914)

XV CORPS

Gen. von Deimling

30TH DIVISION

60TH BRIGADE
99th & 143rd Regts.
85TH BRIGADE
105th & 136th Regts.

39TH DIVISION

61ST BRIGADE
126th & 132nd Regts.
82ND BRIGADE
171st & 172nd Regts.

II BAVARIAN CORPS

Gen von. Martini

3RD BAVARIAN DIV.

5TH BAVARIAN BRIGADE
22nd & 23rd Bavarian Regts.
6TH BAVARIAN BRIGADE
17th & 18th Bavarian Regts.

4TH BAVARIAN DIV.

7TH BAVARIAN BRIGADE
5th & 9th Bavarian Regts.
5TH BAVARIAN RESERVE BRIGADE
5th & 8th Bavarian Resere Regts.

26TH DIVISION (SEE XIII CORPS)

GROUP GEROK

6TH BAVARIAN RESERVE DIVISION (SEE XIV RESERVE CORPS)
3RD DIVISION (SEE II CORPS)
25TH RESERVE DIVISION (SEE XIII CORPS)
11TH LANDWEHR DIVISION

ARMY GROUP LINSINGEN

(8-18 Nov. 1914)

XV CORPS

(see Army Group Fabeck)

PLETENBERG'S CORPS

4TH DIVISION

(see II Corps)

WINCKLER'S COMPOSITE GUARD DIVISION

2ND GUARD BRIGADE
2nd & 3th Foot Guard Regts.
4TH GUARD BRIGADE
2nd & 4th Guard Grenadier Regts.

CAVALRY

(As organized 20 Oct. 1914)

I CAV. CORPS

Lt. Gen. von Richtofen

GUARD CAV. DIVISION

Maj.Gen.von Etzel

4TH CAV. DIVISION

Lt.Gen. von Garnier

II CAV. CORPS

Gen. von der Marwitz

2ND CAV. DIVISION

Maj.Gen. Thumb von Neuburg

7TH CAV. DIVISION

Lt. Gen. von Heydebreck

IV CAV. CORPS

Lt.Gen. von Hollen

6TH CAV. DIVISION

Lt.Gen. Egon von Smettow

9TH CAV. DIVISION

Maj.Gen. Eberhard von Smettow

V CAVALRY CORPS

Lt.Gen. von Stetton

3RD CAV. DIVISION

Lt.Gen. von Unger

BAVARIAN CAV. DIVISION

Lt. Gen. von Wenniger

Note: A German cavalry division consisted of three cavalry brigades, each of two regiments; one horse artillery group, one machine gun squadron, one wireless signal section, one engineer detachment, one or two Jäger battalions.

THE OPPOSING PLANS

Despite the impasse on the Western Front in the autumn of 1914, many people still considered that the war could be finished quickly. A wide corridor, free of the German invader, ran down the coast of Belgium and France. There were 170 miles of open country from the River Oise northwards to the Channel coast unoccupied by the Germans as it was outside their invasion route. Antwerp, Zeebrugge, Ostend and the French Channel ports were in full use by the Allies and only scattered detachments of Allied troops protected the corridor. The solution for both sides was identical: outflank the enemy, exploit the gain and victory was certain. Thus, the Flanders battle lines moved remorselessly towards the coast in the so-called 'race to the sea', in reality the inevitable result of sound military principles.

THE BEF IN FLANDERS 8–11 OCTOBER 1914

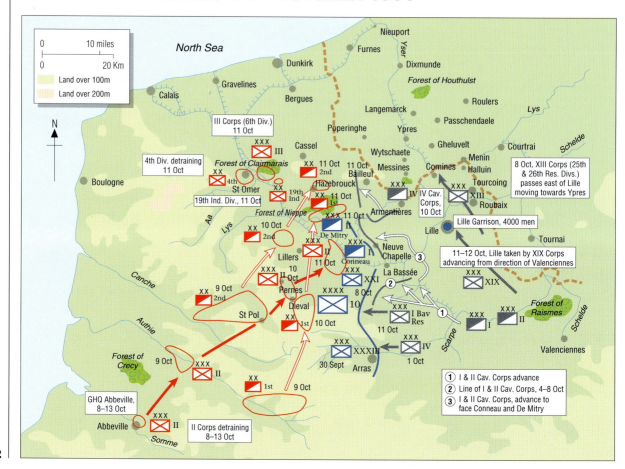

THE GERMAN PLAN

Colonel-General Erich von Falkenhayn became Chief of the German General Staff on 14 September. He quickly decided that the war could be won in Flanders and his plan consisted of three separate operations. One would be a major assault towards Arras; the second, a cavalry sweep across Flanders to the coast; or thirdly, taking Antwerp. Occupying the coastal corridor would lead to the fall of Zeebrugge and Ostend. Ypres, the most westerly town in Belgian Flanders and a vital communications centre, would come next, followed by Nieuport, Dunkirk, Boulogne and Calais. Germany would control access to the Channel and England itself could be invaded.

It was a heady prospect. Calais, not Paris, now became the glittering prize, possession of which would win the war on the Western Front.

THE ALLIED PLANS

Both French and British had their own thoughts on what to do, but they had a common purpose – to drive the enemy from France and Belgium. Joffre concentrated on outflanking the foe. Each attempt was parried; each German effort, in turn, was countered by the French. When Sir John French proposed moving the BEF, he and Joffre agreed that the British would concentrate close to Lille and outflank the German line. They would then push deep into Belgium in a rapid deployment to bring the war to a victorious conclusion.

French had not been entirely honest with Joffre. Winston Churchill, First Lord of the Admiralty, had visited French on 27 September to discuss proposals both for reinforcing Antwerp and landing a large British force at Zeebrugge or Ostend to attack the Germans in the flank – plans rather different from those mentioned to Joffre. Churchill had already sent a Royal Marine Brigade to Dunkirk on 12 September. It was a feeble force, about 2,000 strong, whose officers were either aged or inexperienced. The men were mostly pensioned reservists, together with 700 recruits who had never fired a rifle.

Their plans changed, however, when the Germans attacked Antwerp on 29 September. The Belgian High Command informed the British Government on 30 October that, unless substantial reinforcements arrived, they would have to evacuate Antwerp. The British at once sent two Naval Brigades, another Churchillian improvisation consisting mostly of sailors untrained in infantry skills. The Royal Marine Brigade which had landed at Dunkirk went on to Antwerp where it arrived on 4 October. Churchill himself, dressed as a Commissioner of

Great things were expected of the Royal Naval Division which was sent to Antwerp. In many contemporary accounts, they had inherited Nelson's genius and it was confidently expected that Antwerp would be held and become a considerable thorn in the German flesh. Unfortunately, the Division had little enough in the way of resources. No khaki was available and the men wore normal working rig. Many of them were neither seamen nor soldiers, the majority being miners from Northumberland and Durham who had volunteered for their county regiments, but for whom there was no equipment. In this picture, they are shown constructing 'elaborate defences' against which it was confidently expected that the German attack would falter.

Trinity House, was there to greet them. He had suggested by telegram to the British Government that he take command of all British troops in Antwerp, but the proposal was hastily declined and Churchill returned to England. More usefully, the 7th Infantry and 3rd Cavalry Divisions, under the command of Lt.Gen. Sir Henry Rawlinson, disembarked at Zeebrugge on 6 October and arrived at Bruges two days later. From there, aided by a French Naval Brigade, they covered the withdrawal of the Belgian garrison from Antwerp shortly before the city surrendered on 10 October. Some of Churchill's volunteers escaped. Others became prisoners or marched north to internment in the Netherlands.

That same day, Sir John French outlined his plans to Gen. Ferdinand Foch, who both commanded the French Army Group North and tried to co-ordinate the efforts of the French, Belgian and British Armies in the area. Foch was an optimist. He believed that the Germans simply did not have the manpower to extend their line to the coast. A vigorous advance would hurl back the foe and win the war within weeks. It would be, Foch assured French, 'a glorious enterprise.'

Sir John French needed little convincing. Foch's optimism simply strengthened his own beliefs: there must be a gap which could be exploited and the BEF would find it. While Antwerp surrendered, French issued a simple order. The BEF would advance to meet the enemy.

His plan received a setback when the Germans occupied Lille on the 11/12 October. The advance would now have to be made towards the north, but the British commander was not disheartened. His army was rapidly getting larger. The Indian Corps would shortly arrive and Rawlinson's command had been transferred to the BEF on 9 October to become IV Corps. Sir John French believed that the enemy were weakening fast and were probably short of men. The 'glorious enterprise' was bound to succeed.

British infantry at Ploegsteert 'Plugstreet' Wood, just north of Armentières in October 1914. They are in defensive positions which are positively luxurious in comparison to some that the BEF manned during the Battle of First Ypres. There is even some barbed wire to be seen as well as sandbags. The photograph is quite possibly of a reserve position.

British stretcher-bearers at work. As with many 1914 photographs, a certain scepticism is necessary. Allegedly showing medical staff at work after a 'short but victorious action', this picture looks too good to be true. Certainly the leg showing in the front right of the picture seems to be wearing the German half-boot, but a number of the casualties appear to be displayed rather more artistically than might be anticipated, given the circumstances.

The Battle of First Ypres lasted from 10 October to 22 November 1914. It was, more precisely, four battles for Ypres; four battles which overlapped and interacted each upon the other. The fighting was confused and the situation complex. Events unfolded simultaneously. Hindsight allows some sort of order. To those who took part, it was more chaotic.

The four recognised battles are: La Bassée (10 October to 2 November); Armentières (13 October to 2 November); Messines (12 October to 2 November); Ypres (19 October to 22 November). The end dates indicate only that the main action had sputtered into a less active phase.

THE BATTLEGROUND

The battle lines ran roughly north to south, from Bixschoote, about five miles north of Ypres, down to Givenchy and La Bassée some 25 or 30 miles to the south. The German Army attacked from the east towards the Channel and North Sea coastline.

The River Lys roughly bisects the battle area, running south-west from Menin for about 14 miles to Armentières, and then a further ten miles to Estaires. La Bassée is 14 miles south of Armentières. The La Bassée canal runs roughly parallel to the Lys for 15 miles before swinging sharply north west, shortly after passing Lille, to join the river.

As a rule of thumb, the La Bassée and Armentières battles took place south of the river; those of Messines and Ypres happened north of it. It is, however, simpler to think of the northern battlefield and the southern battlefield.

The area has been described as a shallow saucer with Ypres at the centre. In what was essentially an artillery war, control of the saucer rim was extremely important. Seven miles south of Ypres, at Messines, begins a ridge, about 200 feet at its highest point. It runs two miles north to Wytschaete before a curve north-east then takes in places once notorious to British ears – Hollebeke, Zillebeke, Sanctuary Wood, Hill 60, Gheluvelt, Windhoek, Nonnebosschen, Polygon Wood, Broodseinde, Passchendaele, Langemarck, Bixschoote. This was the infamous Salient, never quiet, always dangerous. The First Battle of Ypres became an agonising struggle to control this ridge, which is only three miles from the town at its closest point. It gave a view over the whole Flanders plain, a view which allowed gunners to shell targets with devastating accuracy. Sir John French, however, was in no mood to consider defensive battles for minor ridges near provincial Belgian towns when he prepared his orders for the 10 October 1914. The cavalry and II Corps were already in position and III Corps nearly so. I Corps would soon be clear of the Aisne. Indian troops had already landed at Marseilles. Clearly, the BEF would easily sweep aside the minor enemy forces, probably cavalry, which Sir John believed were all that stood between him and the liberation of Belgium.

Operation Order No. 33 thus began with a touch of Sir John's unbounded optimism. 'It is the intention of the Commander-in-Chief to advance to meet the enemy, prolonging the French left'. They were bold words in tune with brave thoughts that the war would soon be won. 'The Marshal wishes at all costs to go to Brussels,' wrote Foch to Joffre. 'I shall not hold him back.'

Von Falkenhayn, Crown Prince Rupprecht and Grand Duke Albrecht had their own ideas. They contemplated a day when the black-crossed regimental flags of the German Army would flutter in a victorious wind as their soldiers paraded through the streets of Calais.

LA BASSÉE AND GIVENCHY, 12–14 OCTOBER

The two divisions of II Corps, concentrated at Bèthune, began the offensive on 12 October with an apparently simple task. They were to move north-east to relieve the French before advancing to the line of the La Bassée road between the two villages of Lorgies and Estaires. They were to maintain contact with the French at Vermelles to the south, and anticipated only negligible opposition.

The task was not as easy as it seemed. Ominous signs suggested that the enemy strength was more than a just few cavalrymen. On the 11th, an intercepted German wireless message referred to an impending attack from Lille towards Bèthune. The same day, the French cavalry in front of II Corps were pushed back south of the La Bassée canal, and more seriously, the French lost Vermelles that night in a sharp and savage action.

The morning was cold and foggy. II Corps went forward in extended formation across patchwork fields and hedgerows, along narrow lanes fringed with vegetation, passing huddled farmsteads and through small villages with tiny churches. Behind the hedges, in the church towers, in the lofts of barns, German Jaegers and dismounted cavalry, supported by artillery, waited. These were men who had met the British at Mons and Le Cateau and suffered for it. It was now their turn to show how good they were.

Nowhere was there much above a skirmish; the firing sputtered lazily into life like a cheap firework set piece. Marksmen picked targets. German horse artillery shelled the long line of British soldiers who hugged any cover they could find and casualty numbers crept upwards. By dusk, the objective of the La Bassée-Estaires-Lorgies road had not been reached. Indeed, there had been no advance at all in many places from the positions held by the French.

One single action sums up the whole. The 1st Dorsets relieved French Territorials at the hamlet of Pont Fixe on the north bank of the La Bassée canal, a village about three miles west of the day's objective. 'D' Company advanced on the northern side of the canal, 'A' Company kept pace on the other bank, following a railway track alongside the canal. They had only just started when a message came from 15th Brigade headquarters. There was to be an attack along the whole line, in concert with the French, at 1500 that afternoon.

Thirty minutes before the planned attack, there was no sign of any movement. The battalion pickets reported enemy activity as small groups of Jaegers probed forward. A few prisoners were taken in ill-tempered skirmishes. The Dorsets' commander, Lt.Col. L. J. Bols, decided to press

These two photographs show the arrival of the first British troops – men of the 3rd Cavalry Division – in Ypres on 13 October 1914. Ypres was functioning normally and the population turned out in force to gaze at the new arrivals. In the days that followed the arrival of the BEF, many shopkeepers in Ypres did excellent business – these photographs rapidly made their appearance as postcards – and more than one soldier took the advice of a sergeant-major to 'git yer 'air cut while you 'as a chance.'

The Dream. Few illustrations in the British press, or indeed elsewhere, gave any indication of the reality of the war that was happening on the Western Front. Many of the pictures that did appear were either romanticised artists' impressions or carefully presented photographs, posed especially for the camera. This picture of Indian troops is typical. Although probably taken in France, its claim to show Indian troops preparing to advance on enemy positions is less than accurate.

on. There was no covering artillery fire, but a machine gun was mounted on a factory roof to support 'A' & 'D' Companies. About a mile ahead were some railway sidings, partially screened by masses of stacked bricks two or three hundred yards before the sidings. Enemy soldiers were seen moving up to the scattered heaps of bricks. The British machine gun fired calculated bursts as the wary Dorsets advanced.

The British cleared a few enemy outposts either side of the canal before reaching open ground. Almost immediately, both companies came under fire from their right and from the brickstacks. German troops were concealed 800 yards away in the village of Cuinchy on the British flank, as well as among the bricks. There was little cover. 'A' Company was in a field of harvest stubble, 'D' Company among root crops. The British dropped to their faces and found shelter where they could. At dusk, the Dorsets disengaged. There were 43 casualties including 11 killed and two missing.

Despite the show of enemy strength, GHQ orders that night were still optimistic. It was 'the Commander-in-Chief's intention to continue the advance, passing the army to the north of Lille and driving the enemy before it.' Sir John French saw no problem in advancing 12 miles on a seven-mile wide frontage and, incidentally, capturing Armentières. Unaware that his advance had foundered, Sir John still thought that the Germans were outnumbered and withdrawing. He did not realise that the enemy was in strong defences and was being steadily reinforced.

II Corps faced the German I, II and IV Cavalry Corps. Smith–Dorrien's orders were much as before; a thin line of khaki would advance at first light. There was no specific artillery support; the gunners would fire as and when they could in support of the infantry.

Again, the Dorsets provide a vivid, if slightly extreme, example of the day's action. They began their dawn advance shrouded by a mist that obscured their movements from the enemy Guard Cavalry, who were supported by Jaegers and artillery, as well as more dismounted cavalry units. The German guns included heavy howitzers.

The mist gave way to a grey, cloudy day and the Dorsets came under steady and prolonged fire. They advanced some 2,000 yards, again supported by their single machine gun, but reinforced this time by two 18-pdr. field guns. There was no sign of any advance on the south side of the canal; on the Dorsets' left, the 1st Bedfords, holding the village of Givenchy, also failed to move. This was easy to explain. The Dorsets could see and hear for themselves the ferocious artillery and small arms fire that had pinned down the Bedfords since dawn. One platoon was wiped out by two howitzer shells in quick succession, and by noon the battalion was virtually without officers.

Rain came at midday. The Dorsets' position became precarious. They had captured or killed more than 80 German

A British machine gun in action. Although allegedly portraying a Maxim machine gun crew in action during 1914, this is probably another posed photograph. Its interest, though, lies in the original caption which lays stress on the importance of the machine gun as a defensive weapon. One of the enduring myths about the First World War is that 'the generals' on the British side failed to recognise the importance of machine guns whereas the Germans did. The British establishment of machine guns in 1914 was precisely that of the German Army and would, indeed, have been higher if the Treasury had not vetoed plans for even greater numbers.

soldiers as they advanced, but were still under heavy fire from their right flank and from the brickstacks. They were also the targets of a German howitzer battery. The two British 18-pdrs. and the machine gun failed to deter a steady build-up of enemy forces.

Matters did not improve. Givenchy was the target of a furious artillery assault for some 30 minutes at about 1330. The Bedfords had already fought off two infantry attacks and they now received a third. Two German Jaeger battalions, supported by dismounted cavalry, fell upon them. Bitter and savage hand-to-hand fighting forced the sorely out-numbered British from Givenchy. 11 Battery of the RFA lost two guns as the jubilant Germans stormed down the village street.

This withdrawal isolated the Dorsets, who suffered a further attack from the right which knocked out the machine gun. To their front, the German troops among the bricks maintained a persistent harassing fire. A mass of enemy soldiers began to advance from Givenchy while another large force approached from the left rear.

Retreat was unpalatable, but inevitable. The movement had hardly started when the German infantry arrived in force. In bloody fighting, the 18 pdr. gun crews fired as if they were operating machine guns, but all became casualties as the position was overwhelmed. Most of the wounded were taken prisoner, but a dozen or so managed to evade the enemy and crawl back to safety during the night, among them, Col. Bols.

The 1st Bedfords lost 117 men at Givenchy; the Dorsets had a casualty list of 399, of whom 148 were killed.

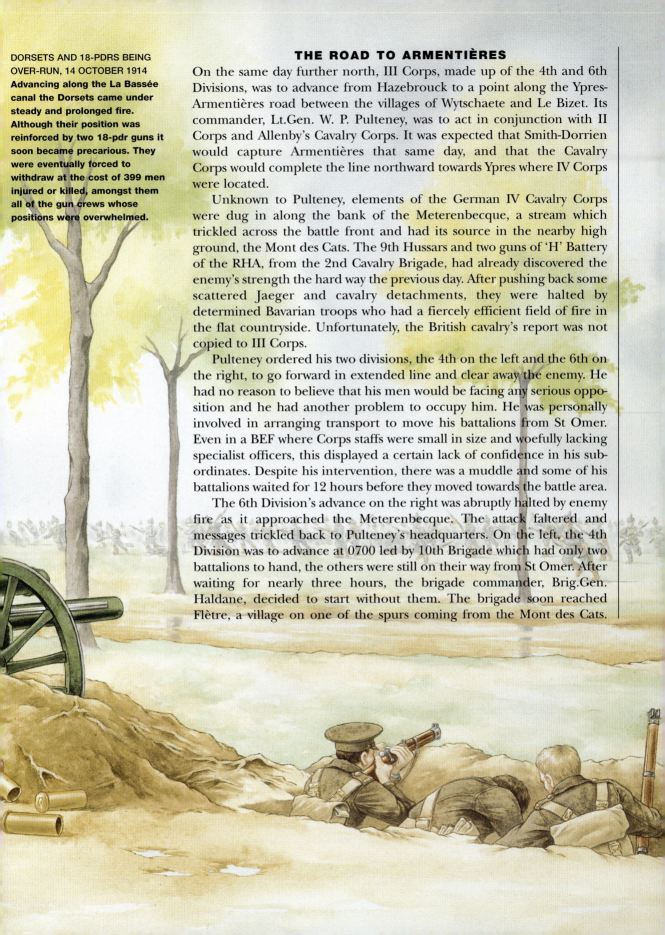

THE ROAD TO ARMENTIÈRES

On the same day further north, III Corps, made up of the 4th and 6th Divisions, was to advance from Hazebrouck to a point along the Ypres-Armentières road between the villages of Wytschaete and Le Bizet. Its commander, Lt.Gen. W. P. Pulteney, was to act in conjunction with II Corps and Allenby's Cavalry Corps. It was expected that Smith-Dorrien would capture Armentières that same day, and that the Cavalry Corps would complete the line northward towards Ypres where IV Corps were located.

Unknown to Pulteney, elements of the German IV Cavalry Corps were dug in along the bank of the Meterenbecque, a stream which trickled across the battle front and had its source in the nearby high ground, the Mont des Cats. The 9th Hussars and two guns of 'H' Battery of the RHA, from the 2nd Cavalry Brigade, had already discovered the enemy's strength the hard way the previous day. After pushing back some scattered Jaeger and cavalry detachments, they were halted by determined Bavarian troops who had a fiercely efficient field of fire in the flat countryside. Unfortunately, the British cavalry's report was not copied to III Corps.

Pulteney ordered his two divisions, the 4th on the left and the 6th on the right, to go forward in extended line and clear away the enemy. He had no reason to believe that his men would be facing any serious opposition and he had another problem to occupy him. He was personally involved in arranging transport to move his battalions from St Omer. Even in a BEF where Corps staffs were small in size and woefully lacking specialist officers, this displayed a certain lack of confidence in his subordinates. Despite his intervention, there was a muddle and some of his battalions waited for 12 hours before they moved towards the battle area.

The 6th Division's advance on the right was abruptly halted by enemy fire as it approached the Meterenbecque. The attack faltered and messages trickled back to Pulteney's headquarters. On the left, the 4th Division was to advance at 0700 led by 10th Brigade which had only two battalions to hand, the others were still on their way from St Omer. After waiting for nearly three hours, the brigade commander, Brig.Gen. Haldane, decided to start without them. The brigade soon reached Flètre, a village on one of the spurs coming from the Mont des Cats.

According to this photograph the British Army copied the Belgian idea of arranging supplies of dogs to pull machine guns! The author's research to date has failed to establish the truth of this claim. The rumour current in the BEF was that the dogs bolted, complete with the guns, as soon as any shelling started.

The British cavalry there told Haldane that the enemy occupied Meteren, a village two miles to the south and that Germans had also been seen on another spur of high ground between Flètre and Meteren.

It was nearly noon, misty, with a light rain. Haldane sent forward the 1st Royal Warwicks. It could have been a pre-war exercise on Salisbury Plain until German artillery came into action. Haldane ordered his own gunners to retaliate.

Maj.Gen. de Lisle, commanding the 1st Cavalry Division arrived to launch a brigade attack against Fontaine Houck, a village about two miles to the east. If Haldane pressed on to Meteren, the capture of both villages would outflank the Germans along the Meterenbecque.

The Warwicks made excellent progress. They quickly cleared some Jaeger detachments from the spur and were at the head of the Meteren-becque by 1300. Their leading companies cautiously began to advance into Meteren itself.

At about the same time, air reconnaissance reported that 500 enemy troops had reinforced Meteren. This news, combined with the messages from the 6th Division at the Meterenbecque, was sufficient to sharpen Pulteney's apprehensions of failure. He promptly decided that only an attack by his full Corps would be strong enough to drive back the Germans.

The Warwicks' success was instantly dissipated. Gen. Snow, commanding the 4th Division, ordered the Warwicks' withdrawal. Ironically, the order arrived just as the enemy was evacuating Meteren. As the British pulled out, the Germans quickly re-occupied the village and harried the retreating troops with heavy small arms fire. Casualties soared. The Warwicks lost only 11 men on the approach to Meteren; by the time they had completed their withdrawal, the casualty list contained 246 names.

The III Corps attack did not start until 1515 – it took time to write orders and move battalions. Meteren and Fontaine Houck were not occupied until after dark. In both cases, the defence prudently withdrew as the full weight of the assault was revealed.

TROOP MOVEMENTS

While both II Corps and III Corps endured a frustrating day, the British cavalry to the north made some interesting discoveries during its actions along the high ground that ran into Belgium. The 2nd Cavalry Division, under Maj.Gen. Hubert Gough, had been very busy. They had taken Mont Noir by early evening and patrols were sent on to Mont Kemmel. Some of De Lisle's men from the 1st Cavalry Division moved towards the long spur of Neuve Eglise, by-passing the German-held town of Bailleul to do so. It was a night of heavy rain and the scattered Germans who saw them exaggerated the British strength when they reported back.

Their presence, allied with the fall of Meteren and Fontaine Houck, caused a hasty withdrawal by the German 3rd Cavalry Division and its supporting infantry from Bailleul. Fearing that the main road to Armentières would be cut, the Germans retired. Further north, the British 3rd Cavalry Division from Rawlinson's IV Corps had clattered across the cobblestones of the Grand Place at Ypres that afternoon. The next day the 7th Division joined them, ready to be deployed eastward against Menin, Courtrai and Roulers. To Sir John French, it was clear that everything was coming together very satisfactorily indeed.

Another grey dawn on 14 October found III Corps' units eager to pursue the enemy, but orders came. During the night, Smith-Dorrien had asked Sir John French for a division from III Corps to reinforce him. Pulteney responded, reasonably enough, by pointing out that the best way to help Smith-Dorrien was for III Corps to continue to advance around Lille. This would pull German troops away from the II Corps area as the enemy flank was threatened. This all took time and it was not until late afternoon that III Corps began to advance on Bailleul, and it

British artillery and French cavalry pass on a road south of Ypres. This is a good road and reasonably wide – many others were far less amenable for good communication.

SIR JOHN'S OFFENSIVE, 12–20 OCTOBER 1914

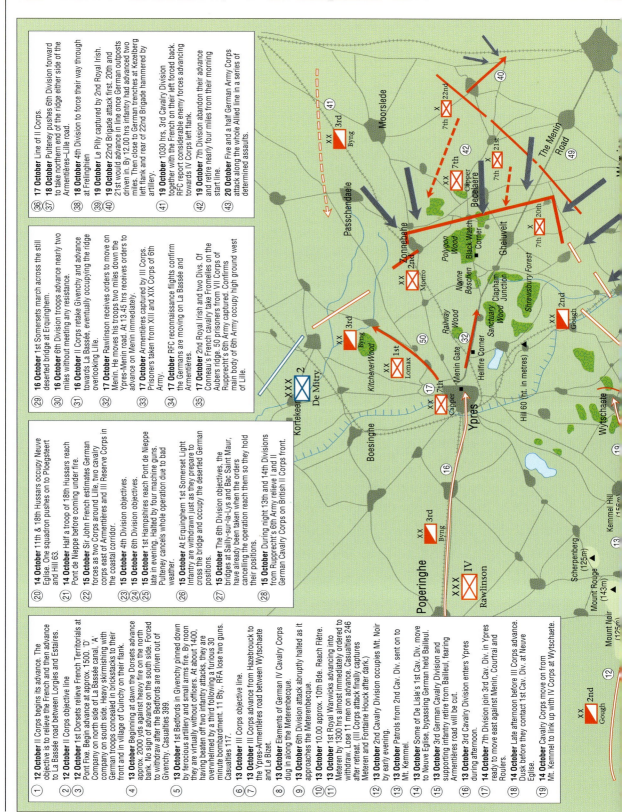

① **12 October** II Corps begins its advance. The objective is to relieve the French and then advance to La Bassée road between Lorgies and Estaires.

② **12 October** II Corps objective line

③ **12 October** 1st Dorsets relieve French Territorials at Pont Fixe. Begin advance at approx. 1500. 'D' Company on north side of La Bassée canal. 'A' company on south side. Heavy skirmishing with German troops concealed in brickstacks to their front and in village of Cuinchy on their flank.

④ **13 October** Beginning at dawn the Dorsets advance approx. 2000 yds against heavy fire on the north bank. No sign of advance on the south side. Forced to withdraw after the Bedfords are driven out of Givenchy. Casualties 399.

⑤ **13 October** 1st Bedfords in Givenchy pinned down by ferocious artillery and small arms fire. By noon they are virtually without officers. At about 1400, having beaten off two infantry attacks, they are overwhelmed by a third following a furious 30 minute bombardment. 11 Bty., RFA lose two guns. Casualties 117.

⑥ **13 October** III Corps objective line.

⑦ **13 October** III Corps advance from Hazebrouck to the Ypres-Armentières road between Wytschaete and Le Bizet.

⑧ **13 October** Elements of German IV Cavalry Corps dug in along the Meterenbecque.

⑨ **13 October** 6th Division attack abruptly halted as it approaches the Meterenbecque.

⑩ **13 October** 10.00 approx. 10th Bde. Reach Flêtre.

⑪ **13 October** 1st Royal Warwicks advancing into Meteren by 1300 hrs almost immediately ordered to withdraw. Lose 11 men on advance. Casualties 246 after retreat. (III Corps attack finally captures Meteren and Fontaine Houck after dark.)

⑫ **13 October** 2nd Cavalry Division occupies Mt. Noir by early evening.

⑬ **13 October** Patrols from 2nd Cav. Div. sent on to Mt. Kemmel.

⑭ **13 October** Some of De Lisle's 1st Cav. Div. move to Neuve Eglise, bypassing German held Bailleul.

⑮ **13 October** 3rd German Cavalry Division and supporting infantry retire from Bailleul, fearing Armentières road will be cut.

⑯ **13 October** 3rd Cavalry Division enters Ypres during afternoon.

⑰ **14 October** 7th Division join 3rd Cav. Div. in Ypres ready to move east against Menin, Courtrai and Roulers.

⑱ **14 October** Late afternoon before III Corps advance. Dusk before they contact 1st Cav. Div. at Neuve Eglise.

⑲ **14 October** Cavalry Corps move on from Mt. Kemmel to link up with IV Corps at Wytschaete.

⑳ **14 October** 11th & 18th Hussars occupy Neuve Eglise. One squadron pushes on to Ploegsteert and Hill 63.

㉑ **14 October** Half a troop of 18th Hussars reach Pont de Nieppe before coming under fire.

㉒ **15 October** Sir John French estimates German forces as two Corps around Lille, two cavalry corps east of Armentières and III Reserve Corps in the coastal corridor.

㉓ **15 October** 4th Division objectives.

㉔ **15 October** 6th Division objectives.

㉕ **15 October** 1st Hampshires reach Pont de Nieppe late in evening. Halted by four machine guns. Pulteney cancels whole operation due to bad weather.

㉖ **15 October** At Erquinghem 1st Somerset Light Infantry are withdrawn just as they prepare to cross the bridge and occupy the deserted German positions.

㉗ **15 October** The 6th Division objectives, the bridges at Sailly-sur-la-Lys and Bac Saint Maur, have already been taken when the orders cancelling the operation reach them so they hold their positions.

㉘ **15 October** During night 13th and 14th Divisions from Rupprecht's 6th Army relieve I and II German Cavalry Corps on British II Corps front.

㉙ **16 October** 1st Somersets march across the still deserted bridge at Erquinghem.

㉚ **16 October** 6th Division troops advance nearly two miles without meeting any resistance.

㉛ **16 October** II Corps retake Givenchy and advance towards La Bassée, eventually occupying the ridge overlooking Lille.

㉜ **17 October** Rawlinson receives orders to move on Menin. He moves his troops two miles down the Ypres-Menin road. At 13.45 hrs receives orders to advance on Menin immediately.

㉝ **17 October** Armentières captured by III Corps. Prisoners taken from XIII and XIX Corps of 6th Army.

㉞ **17 October** RFC reconnaissance flights confirm the Germans are moving on La Bassée and Armentières.

㉟ **17 October** 2nd Royal Irish and two Divs. Of Conneau's French cavalry take Fromelles on the Aubers ridge. 50 prisoners from VII Corps captured. Confirms main body of 6th Army occupy high ground west of Lille.

㊱ **17 October** Line of II Corps.

㊲ **18 October** Pulteney pushes 6th Division forward to take northern end of the ridge either side of the Armentières-Lille road.

㊳ **18 October** 4th Division to force their way through at Frelinghien.

㊴ **19 October** Le Pilly captured by 2nd Royal Irish.

㊵ **19 October** 22nd Brigade attack first. 20th and 21st would advance in line once German outposts driven in. By 12.00 hrs infantry had advanced two miles. Then close to German trenches at Kezelberg left flank and rear of 22nd Brigade hammered by artillery.

㊶ **19 October** 1030 hrs, 3rd Cavalry Division together with the French on their left forced back. RFC report considerable enemy forces advancing towards IV Corps left flank.

㊷ **19 October** 7th Division abandon their advance and retire nearly four miles from their morning start line.

㊸ **20 October** Five and a half German Army Corps attack along the whole Allied line in a series of determined assaults.

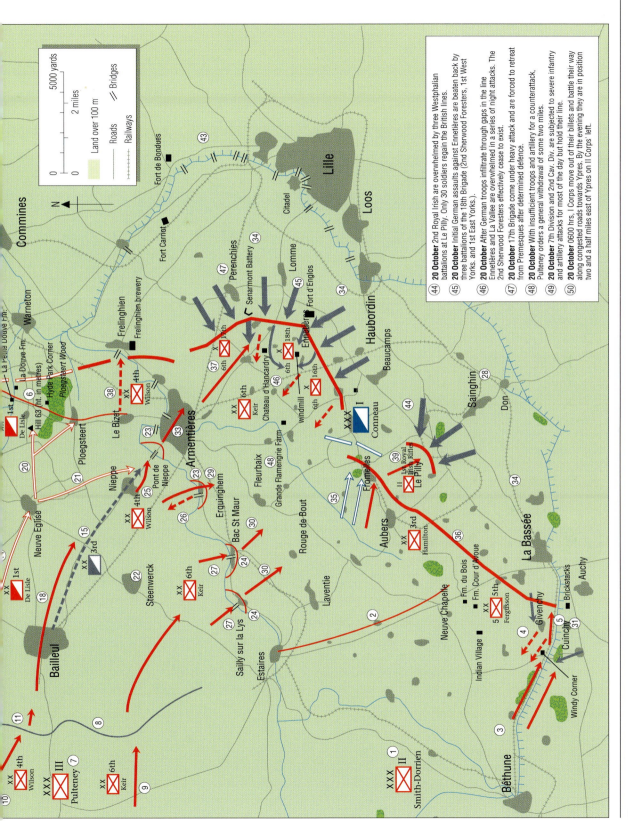

Commines

Warneton

La Petite Douve Fm.

1st De Lisle

Hill 63 (ht. in metres)

Hyde Park Corner

Ploegsteert Wood

Frelinghien

Frelinghien brewery

Le Bizet

4th Wilson

Ploegsteert

Fort de Bondues

43

Lille

Loos

Fort Carnot

Citadel

47

Perenchies **34**

Senarmont Battery

Lomme

Fort d'Englos **34**

45

Ennetières

Haubordin

Beaucamps

17th **6th**

37

6th Keir

X Chateau d'Hancardry

18th **6th**

windmill

X **6th** **16th**

Sainghin **28**

44

I Conneau

XXX **I**

Don **34**

Nieppe

23

33

Armentières

23 **29**

Erquinghem

25 **4th** Wilson

26

38

XX 6th Keir

Fleurbaix

Grande Flamengrie Farm.

48

Rouge de Bout

35

Aubers

Fromelles

39 **II** 1st Royal Irish Rifle

Le Pilly

3rd Hamilton.

XX **3rd**

36

La Bassée

Bac St Maur

30

27 **24**

30

24

22 **Steenwerck**

XX 6th Keir

27

Sailly sur la Lys

Laventie

Neuve Chapelle

Fm. du Bois

Fm. Cour d'Avoue

5th Fergtbsson

5 **XX**

Indian Village

Windy Corner

Cuinchy

Brickstacks

5 **31**

Auchy

Givenchy

4

Estaires

2

3

Béthune

15

Neuve Eglise

3rd

XX **3rd** De Lisle

XX 1st De Lisle

18

20

21

Bailleul

11

8

10

XX 4th Wilson

XXX III Pulteney **7**

XX 6th Keir **9**

1

XXX II Smith-Dorrien

35

Map legend:

5000 yards
2 miles

0

Land over 100 m
Roads
Bridges
Railways

N

(44) **20 October** 2nd Royal Irish are overwhelmed by three Westphalian battalions at Le Pilly. Only 30 soldiers regain the British lines.

(45) **20 October** Initial German assaults against Ennetières are beaten back by three battalions of the 18th Brigade (2nd Sherwood Foresters, 1st West Yorks. and 1st East Yorks.).

(46) **20 October** After German troops infiltrate through gaps in the line Ennetières and La Vallee are overwhelmed in a series of night attacks. The 2nd Sherwood Foresters effectively cease to exist.

(47) **20 October** 17th Brigade come under heavy attack and are forced to retreat from Premesques after determined defence.

(48) **20 October** With insufficient troops and artillery for a counterattack, Pulteney orders a general withdrawal of some two miles.

(49) **20 October** 7th Division and 2nd Cav. Div. are subjected to severe infantry and artillery attacks for most of the day but hold their line.

(50) **20 October** 0600 hrs, I Corps move out of their billets and battle their way along congested roads towards Ypres. By the evening they are in position two and a half miles east of Ypres on II Corps' left.

Indian troops in trenches. Taken on the Messines Ridge in November 1914, this photograph vividly shows these soldiers are suffering grievously from the cold and damp. A contemporary observer noted how the 'Indians were grey with the cold' and their fighting abilities and endurance were finally much hampered by the depressing winter weather in Europe.

was dusk by the time the 4th Division made contact with 1st Cavalry Division troopers on the Neuve Eglise spur.

In the south, II Corps held its line, digging-in against any enemy attack. Smith-Dorrien was content to wait for Pulteney to make ground. The Cavalry Corps continued to be active. They moved on from Mount Kemmel and linked up with IV Corps at Wytschaete. The 11th and 18th Hussars occupied Neuve Eglise and one squadron reached Hill 63 and Ploegsteert.

That night, a half-troop of the 18th Hussars went south and reached the Pont de Nieppe, where the road to Armentières crossed the Lys, before being challenged and coming under fire. Their report that the Germans were withdrawing to Armentières, allied with the occupation of Wytschaete, Hill 63 and Ploegsteert convinced GHQ that the enemy was pulling back to avoid being cut off by a turning movement from the north. It looked as if the war would soon be over.

The same evening, the last of a long procession of trains hissed to a halt at a country station west of Brussels. The German troops who got out had clean uniforms, bright equipment and polished boots. They were the enthusiastic 'August volunteers' who now formed XXII, XXIII, XXVI and XXVII Corps and were en route to the Fourth Army. Von Falkenhayn's plans were gathering pace.

RELUCTANT ADVANCE, 15–18 OCTOBER

III Corps stayed put on the morning of 15 October and at noon, Sir John French consulted with Pulteney and Allenby at III Corps Headquarters. Information from patrols, confirmed by RFC reports, was that the enemy was withdrawing between Armentières and Menin, so French promptly issued new orders.

The BEF would advance eastwards, 'attacking the enemy wherever met'. II Corps was to capture La Bassée and advance on Lille whilst III Corps occupied Armentières and then moved eastward. The Cavalry Corps would cover the left flank. IV Corps was to advance in the direction of Menin, Courtrai and Roulers. Enemy forces were estimated at two corps around Lille; two cavalry corps east of Armentières; and III Reserve Corps, which had besieged Antwerp, in the coastal corridor.

Gallieni had used taxis to transport soldiers to the front at the Battle of the Marne. The BEF went one better. In October 1914, the London General Omnibus Company, among others, handed over vehicles, complete with volunteer drivers, to go to Flanders. The drivers were given a swift medical examination, issued with uniforms and rifles and a civilian raincoat in lieu of a greatcoat. The buses arrived in their civilian livery and were painted grey or khaki as opportunity provided. Each brigade was allocated 30 vehicles. One soldier of the London Scottish recalled that the bus which took him to Ypres was the same one, with the same driver, who had taken him to work each morning before the war! This photograph shows troops in London riding in a bus commandeered for general transport purposes. The novelty was such that the Germans themselves featured the use of the London buses – below is a photograph which appeared in a German publication with a grudging acknowledgement of British ingenuity!

Pulteney ordered the 4th and 6th Divisions to capture four bridges across the Lys. The 4th Division would secure the Pont de Nieppe and the bridge at Erquinghem; on their right, the 6th Division would take the bridge at Bac Saint Maur and its close neighbour a mile upstream at Sailly.

The 1st Hampshires were allocated the Pont de Nieppe. It was after six in the evening and dark when they set off. As they approached the bridge, they came under machine gun fire and took a dozen or so casualties. Scrambling for cover, (one platoon commander sadly choosing a cesspit as a refuge) they quickly established that four machine guns were firing from the opposite bank. As the Hampshires pondered how to proceed orders arrived from brigade postponing the attack. Gen. Pulteney had reverted to caution. He considered the weather, fog and rain too risky for a night advance and cancelled the operation.

The 1st Somerset Light Infantry at Erquinghem were withdrawn just as they prepared to cross the bridge and occupy deserted German positions. The 6th Division units had already taken their bridges at Bac Saint Maur and Sailly before the orders reached them and so they stayed at their posts.

That night, on II Corps front, the German I and II Cavalry Corps were relieved by the 13th and 14th Divisions from the VII Corps of Crown Prince Rupprecht's Sixth Army. On 16 October, Pulteney, after being prodded by GHQ, made sure of his bridgeheads across the Lys. The Somersets marched across the still deserted bridge at Erquinghem and at the Pont de Nieppe, a single round from an 18-pdr. despatched the German defenders. Despite the evidence of a German withdrawal, provided by the 6th Division which advanced nearly two miles without meeting the enemy, Pulteney insisted that the 4th Division should not cross the river until 6th Division had cleared the southern bank.

Further south, Smith-Dorrien's units had produced their own plans for attacking the enemy. They retook Givenchy and advanced once more towards La Bassée, eventually occupying the ridge which overlooked Lille. The next day, Armentières fell to III Corps. The town had been abandoned by the Germans, but a few stragglers were captured. Their identity was a shock to British intelligence. The prisoners were from the XIII and XIX Corps of the Sixth Army, hitherto unknown to the British..

The gap between the right flank of III Corps and the left of Smith Dorrien's II Corps was filled by the French cavalry commanded by Gen. Conneau. Smith-Dorrien had ordered his units to swing south-east. Their right was on the La Bassée canal, their left at Fauquissart six miles to the north. From there, the 2nd Royal Irish, in concert with two divisions of Conneau's cavalry, attacked and took Fromelles on the Aubers Ridge. Fifty prisoners were taken: they came from VII Corps of Rupprecht's Army and they confirmed what the other captives had said – that the main body of the Sixth Army occupied the high ground west of Lille.

The skies cleared that afternoon and RFC aircraft scurried across the front, looking for the enemy. The first report was confirmed by others: there was enemy movement towards La Bassée and Armentières.

Pulteney reacted strongly. On the morning of the 18th, he pushed the 6th Division forward to take the northern end of the ridge, the high ground on either side of the Armentières-Lille road. This would inhibit any German advance. The 4th Division was to force its way through at Frelinghien to the north-west of Lille.

The Belgians held the left of the Allied line and resisted severe German pressure; their artillery was consistently outgunned by superior numbers, but they fought with a rare distinction. Illustrated is a Belgian field gun in action on the Yser front.

By nightfall, after fighting their way through a series of cleverly sited positions held by a well-armed enemy, the 6th Division dug in on the western slope of the ridge. Lille was just over three miles distant, plainly visible to the east. On the right of the line, II Corps was in touch with Conneau's cavalry units who were, in turn, on the right flank of III Corps. Allenby's Cavalry were left of III Corps. The line then ran north to the 7th Division positions astride the road from Ypres to Menin. The 3rd Cavalry Division held the extreme left of the British line.

Rawlinson had received orders the previous day 'to move on Menin' and had advanced his troops two miles along the Ypres-Menin road. They met little resistance, enemy patrols falling back after a few perfunctory shots. At noon, a GHQ liaison officer arrived and expressed bewilderment that Rawlinson had not occupied Menin itself. There was an argument over the meaning of the orders, Rawlinson claiming that 'moving on' was a very different thing to 'attack'. At 1345 that afternoon, a second order arrived in cipher. Converted into plain language , the meaning was stark. IV Corps was to advance immediately on Menin.

Rawlinson still dragged his feet. It was too late to do anything on a rapidly darkening autumn afternoon, but he promised that the 7th Division would move early the next day. Rawlinson was fighting for time. He had already received reports from patrols, refugees and the RFC which suggested that something very nasty was skulking at the far end of the Menin Road.

Smith-Dorrien, Rawlinson and, above all Pulteney, had not displayed great enthusiasm for Sir John's grand offensive. Without actually disobeying orders, an innate caution had impelled them to advance as slowly as they dared; for this, Pulteney, in particular, has been condemned. In the event, this wariness saved the BEF from falling into a trap, and it was close to being sprung.

THE BATTLE OF FIRST YPRES

On Monday 19 October, both the British and German Commanders could feel satisfied about the future. Sir John French was confident that the BEF would continue to advance. II Corps, it was true, had met stiffening resistance near La Bassée, but that town would undoubtedly soon fall. III Corps' advance was also slow, but the opposition they faced could be no more than determined pockets of cavalry. The misunderstanding with Rawlinson had been resolved and Menin would be occupied by lunchtime. Allenby's Cavalry Corps had been rebuffed at the Lys, but this was understandable. They were lightly armed, without the firepower to mount a solid assault. Finally, I Corps had arrived from the Aisne and was assembling at Hazebrouck. British units might even reach the German frontier before the year was out thus bringing the Great European War to a satisfactory end.

For Falkenhayn, the picture seemed equally cheering as the new units arrived. Prince Rupprecht's Sixth Army already faced II Corps and was steadily slowing the British advance. The XIX Corps in Lille had stopped Allenby's cavalry crossing the Lys. Mindful of the strict instructions to remain on the defensive until the attack was launched, they were nonetheless tempting the foe into exposed forward positions which would be annihilated when the time came. III Reserve Corps, the 4th Ersatz, 5th Reserve, and 6th Reserve Divisions had crunched southwards along the coast to Dixmude. They had not merely pursued the retreating Belgians but had screened the arrival of the enthusiastic volunteers of the Fourth Army. On 19 October, these unblooded reinforcements began to close up for the offensive. The same day, III and XXII Corps of Von Beseler's 4th Ersatz Division attacked the joint Belgian and French positions east of the Yser near Dixmude.

Armoured trains had been used in the Second Boer War and they made another appearance in the early days of the First World War. One was crewed by members of the Royal Navy at Antwerp and this rare photograph shows a naval gun mounted on a flat bed behind an armoured locomotive. The picture was taken by a Royal Naval Division member from a troop train – note the sailor looking out of the window, extreme right.

Falkenhayn believed his opponents would be defeated quickly. Ostend was already in German hands. The attack, launched on a line from Arras to the sea, would capture Calais and the other ports, remove the Belgians in their entirety, neutralise the British by cutting the cross-Channel supply lines and thrust at the heart of France. It could all be done before the turn of the year and would bring the Great European War to a satisfactory conclusion.

STRETCHING THE FRONT LINE

Allied action on 19 October started with some promise, but, by nightfall, the line was little changed from the previous evening. Sir John French wanted a vigorous offensive with particular emphasis on taking Menin. The 7th Division was to advance, covered on its left by the 3rd Cavalry Division who were, in turn, to connect with French cavalry at Roulers and the Houthulst Forest. The right flank was protected by the 2nd Cavalry Division and two armoured trains.

The three brigades of the 7th Division faced south-east towards Menin on a five mile front; the 20th Brigade was on the right, close to Kruiseecke, the 21st in the middle by Terhand, and the 22nd on the left opposite Dadizeele. The 22nd Brigade was to attack first. Once it had driven in the German outposts, the other two brigades would advance in line. At first, all went to plan. By noon, the infantry had advanced almost two miles. Then, close to German trenches at Kezelberg, severe artillery fire hammered the left flank and rear of the 22nd Brigade. News of this setback reached Divisional Headquarters almost simultaneously with a message from IV Corps calling off the attack. Rawlinson was reacting to disturbing news. At about 1030, the 3rd Cavalry Division had met strong enemy forces and, together with the French on their left, had been forced back. The RFC then reported concentrations of enemy troops at Gulleghem – only four miles from Menin – and other villages close by. In short, very considerable enemy forces were advancing towards the left flank of IV Corps.

These proud volunteers, from the 45th and 46th Reserve Divisions formed part of the German right. Initially held back by the accurate French 75mm quick-firers, they eventually came into action during the early afternoon. In tight ranks, they advanced towards the village of Hooghlede, across fields of thin stubble interlaced with streams, ditches and wire fences. The officers & NCOs constantly checked the dressing, but the novices found it difficult to keep their set ranks. Artillery and small arms fire lacerated the leading companies until they reached an earth bank, five feet high, behind which they sheltered. Heavily laden with packs and equipment, the first soldiers clambered to the top of the bank, scrabbling at the damp earth, and stood upright to look for the enemy.

French dragoons, covered by the red-brick walls of the village, were 150 metres away. Armed with an inadequate carbine, dismounted French cavalry were not normally lethal. Today, however, they were. Hooghlede eventually fell at dusk. Its defenders retired only after the 51st and 52nd Divisions outflanked them. The 51st Division

The BEF advance north of Ypres was supported on one flank by an armoured train. This photograph shows one of several used in the northern sector, crewed by Belgian soldiers, on its way to the front.

managed to occupy Roulers itself, pushing back the French in a series of disjointed and confusing actions.

Nearer Menin, the left flank of the 3rd Cavalry Division was exposed as the French retreated. The right was similarly opened as the British infantry abandoned its advance and pulled back nearly four miles from their morning start line. The 7th Division lost nearly 200 men during the day, half of whom came from the Welch Fusiliers; the 3rd Cavalry Division took 83 casualties.

Sir John French remained confident. He decided that the German reinforcements were probably going to La Bassée and that north of Ypres there was only a weakened Army Corps. In buoyant mood, he personally told Haig that I Corps, covered by the 3rd Cavalry Division, would advance northwards to capture Bruges and drive the enemy back to Ghent. II Corps and III Corps would continue their offensive. The Cavalry Corps would maintain its positions and the 7th Division entrench. The British commander was heartened to learn that II Corps in the south had captured the hamlet of Le Pilly on the Aubers Ridge. All was going well. French did not believe that the enemy could muster a force of over three and a half corps, and even then this would probably be under-strength, with *Landwehr* divisions of doubtful quality making up the numbers.

On 20 October, a dreary day with mist and drizzle, five-and-a-half German Army Corps erupted against the whole Allied line in a series of determined infantry assaults backed by heavy artillery fire. The numerically superior Germans pressed home their attacks fiercely, achieving considerable local success in some sectors. Sir John had grossly underestimated the opposition.

Life went on much as normal even in villages close to the fighting area. This photograph shows British soldiers passing through a village in October, 1914. Taken probably by a civilian or a British soldier with an illicit camera, this is a picture whose rarity outweighs its dubious quality!

THE GERMAN OFFENSIVE

II Corps were soon in a trying position. The 2nd Royal Irish, who had occupied Le Pilly the previous day, came under strong artillery fire in the early morning before being confronted by three Westphalian battalions drawn from the 16th and 56th Regiments of the Sixth Army's 14th Division. The Royal Irish faced at least three times their own numbers. In mid-afternoon, with no ammunition left, the battalion commander Maj. E. H. Daniell, ordered his men to fix bayonets and counterattack. The few who were unwounded, joined by any others who could walk, charged the approaching enemy through a hail of fire. The Royal Irish lost 17 officers (including Daniell) and 561 men in the whole action: 257 were killed and 290 men taken prisoner. Only 50 of them were unwounded. A mere 30 soldiers evaded the German to regain the British

Another photograph whose lack of quality is compensated by the scene it depicts. This picture shows some of the 7th Division on their arrival at Zeebrugge on the 6th October. A number of soldiers are clearly kilted and are thus of the 2nd Gordons and it is therefore probable that this picture shows part of the 20th Infantry Brigade waiting to entrain – the locomotive in the background has one passenger carriage and a string of goods wagons.

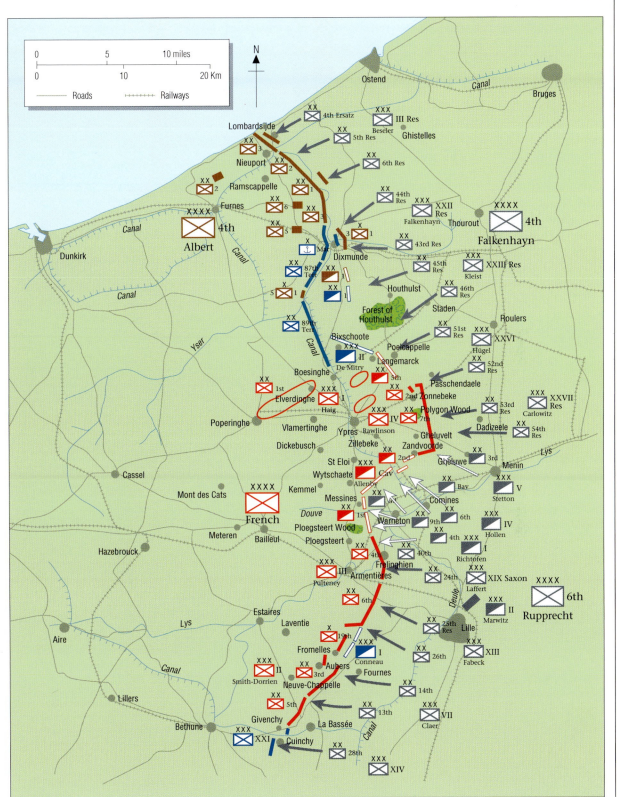

lines. II Corps struggled desperately all day and the German progress was slow and costly.

III Corps also suffered a crushing assault. Pulteney had been alarmed by the reports he had received the previous day and concluded that the Allied advance was floundering and the Germans were preparing to fight. Pulteney thus disregarded Sir John's optimistic instructions and ordered his command to maintain its positions. He further ordered that as many men as possible should form local reserves and that strongpoints should be prepared behind the front line. They were undoubtedly good intentions, but were destined to be thwarted by heavy enemy attacks.

Gen. von Fabeck, commanding the XIII Corps, was ordered to capture Estaires, eight miles to the British rear. His Württemburg and Hessian soldiers were to push forward on a seven mile-wide front, 18 battalions in extended order, advancing towards the ridge which overlooked Lille itself.

The three brigades of the British 6th Division, the 16th, 17th & 18th held the position which ran from Radinghem to Ennetières, thence to Premèsques and Epinette. The 18th Brigade, holding a salient in front of Ennetières, took the brunt of the German assault. At 0700 hours in mist with a drizzling, miserable rain, the British lines came under a severe and sustained artillery bombardment. After an hour, shelling dropped away and the enemy infantry probed forward. The three battalions of the 18th Brigade, the 2nd Sherwood Foresters, 1st West Yorkshire and 1st East Yorkshire had the support of the XXXVIII Brigade of the Royal Field Artillery. Visibility was not good, but although the defenders could see only about 700 yards, the Württemburgers and Hessians suffered grievously. The British soldiers had spent long hours on the range firing at targets 800 yards distant. Many could kill at 1,000 yards and the extended order adopted by an understandably cautious enemy was no protection. The defence was deadly.

Of rather better quality, this photograph was also taken at Zeebrugge on the 6th October; aside from the Belgian soldiers in the foreground, the 7th Division troops are from the 2nd Royal Scots Fusiliers of the 21st Infantry Brigade.

A British 18-pdr. crew ready for action. Although the poses suggest that this photograph may well have been taken specially for publication, examination of the original shows that the crew are alert and handling life ammunition. It does, however contrast sharply with the photograph opposite. Screened from air reconnaissance, this crew was pictured in action in late 1914.

Even so, the British line came under continuing pressure. At about 1100 hours, the Durham Light Infantry went forward in support, just in time to help repulse a determined attack upon the Sherwood Foresters by the 26th Division at 1300 hours. Another German assault, some two hours later, against the right flank was beaten back with heavy enemy losses.

Fabeck, however, had already made other plans. Displeased by the morning's failures, he prepared a night attack to take Ennetières and the hamlets of La Vallée and Le Touquet to the rear and north of the Sherwood Foresters. As the daylight faded, three battalions of German infantry with strong artillery backing fell upon the Foresters. The 11th and 12th Companies of the 122nd Regiment found a gap in the extended British defences and slipped in from the west to the rear of La Vallée. As they prepared to assault the hamlet, they were joined by more troops from their battalion as well as the 2nd Battalion, 125th Regiment who had stormed the positions from the south. The half company of British troops holding La Vallée was severely outnumbered and taken by surprise.

Worse was to come. Troops from the three battalions of the 52nd Infantry Brigade, 25th Reserve Division, threw themselves at the village of Ennetières. The light was poor and the Foresters could not cut down the charging enemy quickly enough. The Germans reached the outskirts of the village and the hastily dug defences. The British soldiers, many abandoning greatcoats and packs, but clutching their rifles and ammunition, scrambled back towards the shelter of their field artillery who were located by a windmill at the north-west end of La Vallée itself.

At the western end of the village, at the cross-roads between Ennetières and La Vallée, the breathless soldiers were relieved to hear men approaching from their rear. These were not reinforcements, however, but the triumphant Germans who had taken La Vallée. In the bruising mêlée that followed, most of the Sherwood Foresters were captured. Two officers and about 60 men fought their way into some houses and held out until the next morning when their ammunition was exhausted. For all practical purposes, the 2nd Sherwood Foresters ceased to exist.

The day's fighting cost the 18th Brigade 1,119 casualties. The defeat of the Sherwood Foresters and the loss of Ennetières caused problems for the East and West Yorkshires on the left of the Foresters and they retired to the west.

To the north, on the left flank of the 18th Brigade, the 17th Brigade also came under attack. The Leinster Regiment held the line Mont de Premèsques–Premèsques–Epinette. They suffered heavy shellfire before facing a fierce infantry charge at Premèsques. Helped by two companies of the East Yorkshires and a company of the North Staffordshires, the Leinsters struggled against far superior numbers but finally retreated, leaving Premèsques to the enemy.

There were neither enough troops nor artillery available to mount a successful counterattack. Pulteney ordered a general withdrawal as far as two miles back from the morning's positions on the right and centre.

I AND IV CORPS REPULSE ATTACKS

In the area of Ypres, IV Corps were, in effect, an advance guard for I Corps and Rawlinson therefore instructed the 7th Division to hold its line at all costs. Soon after midday their left flank came under severe infantry and artillery attack. This assault spread rapidly along the entire 7th Division frontage. It was repulsed, but another came in the late afternoon, this time spreading to the 2nd Cavalry Division on the right of the 7th. The enemy was driven back once more, but had got within 50 yards of the British defences. There were repeated attempts to penetrate the British lines until well after dark.

Kavallerieattacke in der Schlacht bei Ypern.

On the left of the 7th Division, the 3rd Cavalry linked the British and the French positions. The French, in particular de Mitry's Cavalry Corps, faced a series of determined attacks from the XXIII Reserve Corps and were driven out of their positions. This withdrawal exposed the left flank of the British 3rd Cavalry who pulled back in turn. Despite this onslaught, IV Corps reported only 186 casualties for the day.

Sir Douglas Haig was not impressed by grandiose orders to capture Bruges and win the war. He had suspected for some time that GHQ intelligence estimates left much to be desired and had set up his own Intelligence Department in I Corps. Their assessment, together with information from elsewhere, convinced him that he faced a hard fight.

I Corps moved out of its billets on the morning of 20 October at 0600. The troops were hampered by heavily congested roads but, by that evening, were in position some two-and-a-half miles to the east of Ypres to the left of IV Corps. The advance proper would start the next morning. The battle lines for the bloody fighting of First Ypres were slotting into place.

By 21 October Sir John French was at his melancholy worst; breezy optimism had become deep foreboding. Operation Order No 39, however, written the previous evening, was still positive. The II, III and Cavalry Corps and 7th Division were to contain the enemy whilst I Corps was 'to attack vigorously' marching towards Thourout, north of Ypres, and 'attack the enemy wherever met'.

Spirited and imaginative scenes by a variety of artists of the fighting at Ypres were to be found in German, British and French publications. This German postcard depicts a cavalry action between French Cuirassiers and German Lancers in which the Germans are seizing the French unit's tricolour.

The BEF was woefully short of heavy artillery – in sharp contrast to the German army. Here, a 60 pdr. howitzer battery is on the move. Although allegedly taken in France on active service, this picture was almost certainly taken during peace time – the eight-horse teams quickly dwindled to six-horse teams under the pressures of action and re-supply.

Equally romantic and equally inaccurate was this picture of German soldiers assaulting British soldiers, many in red coats and wearing bearskins, grouped under the Union flag. German press accounts at this time are remarkably similar to English ones in their prose and vivid descriptions, most of which are dramatic, but totally false.

News of the reverse at Le Pilly, the loss of Ennetières and La Vallée and the withdrawal of the 6th Division had arrived after midnight with other disquieting information. Air reconnaissance had identified large enemy columns moving towards the front. Very substantial forces indeed opposed the joint Allied line from the Yser to the Lys. French became queasily aware that Falkenhayn might be about to produce a nasty surprise.

When Joffre visited Sir John that day with the welcome news that the French IX Corps was being drafted to Flanders, he quickly discovered that the British commander had reverted to a favourite obsession – the provision of an entrenched camp at Boulogne, a haven to which the BEF could retire if defeated and from which the Royal Navy could transport it back to Britain. Joffre replied bluntly that the idea could not be entertained for even a moment. The invader must be fought and defeated where he stood.

Joffre left, after expressions of goodwill, but with foreboding at the lack of resolution displayed by the British commander. It was fortunate, indeed, that the corps commanders and their subordinates were more steadfast. It was fortunate, too, that they had a keener appreciation of the need to co-operate with their allies, for the coming days would test them sorely.

It is a simple comment on the mercurial way in which Sir John French's mind worked, zooming from despair to euphoria, that, describing the day's events to Kitchener, the BEF commander informed him that 'here and there we were slightly driven back, but our successes predominated', and gave it as his firm opinion that 'the enemy are vigorously playing their last card, and I am confident that they will fail.' It was a sentiment far removed from the wish for a fortress at Boulogne.

Less romantic is this picture of British soldiers somewhere on the Ypres front in 1914; the trench is no more than a deep ditch and there is no wire.

NEW GERMAN TACTICS IN THE SOUTH

It was another cold, dank morning on 21 October, a grim indicator of the winter ahead. Enemy assaults erupted at different points along the 30 miles of Allied positions. In the south, II Corps endured further bitter and savage conflict. Two fresh German units, the 13th and 14th Divisions of the VII Corps were in a pugnacious mood. At about 0700, eleven battalions of German infantry struck the left of the II Corps line, a position held by the 3rd Division. Four British battalions bore the brunt of the attack which was beaten off with fierce rifle and machine gun fire.

The Germans withdrew and when they reappeared it was no longer in mass formation. They used new tactics, forged by bitter combat experience. Small groups of determined and aggressive infantry swarmed forward and kept the defenders on constant alert. This was behaviour far removed from the mass assault and they were tactics at which the German soldier was to become extremely adept.

In the poor visibility, the 2nd South Lancashire were surprised and the enemy forced a gap in the line. They quickly sent reinforcements to exploit their success and it was not until the afternoon that the Germans were finally thrown back and the position stabilised after grim fighting.

II Corps were hard pressed throughout the day – all of the officers of the 1st Duke of Cornwall's Light Infantry became casualties – but every attack was repulsed.

Just to their north, the lightly-armed French cavalry and cyclists of Conneau's command on the left of the 3rd Division were driven back. This exposed the flank. The 3rd Division abandoned its ground, pulling back about a mile. The day's fighting cost II Corps 1,079 officers and men.

The 19th Infantry Brigade formed the southern flank of Pulteney's III Corps and they received the unwelcome attention of heavy shell fire from about 1100 hours as part of the same drive launched against the French and the 3rd Division to their south. In the afternoon, the German infantry attacked, and the fight continued until dark. The Brigade lost about 300 men, many of them wounded, who had to be abandoned when the Brigade finally withdrew. Their defence against superior numbers had been greatly helped by some French horse artillery which had shredded the enemy's left during the attacks.

The rest of III Corps, holding a front about 12 miles long, also endured successive onslaughts. Artillery fire raked their line from early morning onwards. The 12th Brigade on the left of the III Corps line faced the greatest threat. Eight German battalions of the XIX (Saxon) Corps of the Sixth Army, thrust forward in the early hours of the morning. In the mist and dark, they crossed the Lys and advanced towards the village of Le Gheer and Ploegsteert Wood. In a bout of brutal fighting, the 12th Brigade repulsed the initial assaults but continued pressure forced the left of the British line. The Inniskilling Fusiliers were driven back some 400 metres. German troops infiltrated Le Gheer and Ploegsteert Wood from where they enfiladed the British positions to the north and south. A counterattack recovered the lost ground. In the process, 45 Inniskilling Fusiliers who had been taken prisoner were released and 134 Germans surrendered. By dusk, the whole line had been re-established, but 12th Brigade lost 468 officers and men in the fighting. German casualties are not known but 'wherever the enemy had penetrated the front line, the ground was littered with German corpses'.

Elsewhere, III Corps had a relatively quiet day; an attack was mounted against the 6th Division to the south at dusk, but was driven off with heavy enemy losses.

Supplying the BEF was a nightmare. It was simple enough, given the size of the British merchant fleet in 1914, to ship goods to France; once there, however, it became much more difficult. This 1914 scene in a village a few miles behind the lines graphically illustrates the difficulties. It was the same for all the armies and, as the war progressed, more and more ingenious methods were used to try and eliminate logistic bottlenecks.

Somewhere near Ypres. This photograph shows British soldiers in front of a windmill 'being used as an observation post' together with the Belgian civilians who normally worked the mill.

THE NORTHERN BATTLEFIELD: HOLES IN THE LINE

Immediately north of III Corps, Allenby's Cavalry Corps desperately defended one of the most vital pieces of the British front – the Messines Ridge. They had been in action for many days and were agonisingly short of men; one regiment had less than 180 effectives. Under prolonged shelling, with the need to provide sentries and man the pathetic holes which passed for trenches, few managed more than two or three hours sleep each night. The utter weariness and lack of rest caused minds to wander and the simplest orders had to be repeated constantly to men dazed with fatigue.

The two divisions of British cavalry fended off five German cavalry divisions complete with their Jaeger battalions and supporting cyclist infantry. The 1st Cavalry Division on the right of the line dealt with relative ease with attacks from the Guard, 4th and 9th Cavalry Divisions.

The 2nd Cavalry Division had a more wearing day. Heavy shelling forced part of their line to retreat. Against the Bavarian and the 6th Cavalry Division – troops lacking basic infantry skills and without the marksmanship of their opponents – the British held their own. The 3rd Cavalry Brigade, defending without serious problems the village and Château of Hollebeke, received information about its line of retreat *if* such a course of action became necessary. Weary to the point of incomprehension, this was interpreted as an order for instant retirement and the brigade withdrew towards St Eloi, only three miles from Ypres, leaving a wide hole in the British front.

Hubert Gough, commanding the 2nd Cavalry Division, reacted swiftly and ordered his units to restore the line forthwith. They did, but four officers and 11 men became casualties, a telling comment on the lack of spirit shown by the enemy cavalry and the loss of a golden opportunity for the Germans. That night, their commander, Lt. Gen. von Hollen was dismissed.

For the 7th Division, defending nearly six miles of front, the 21st was a brutal day which set the pattern for the remainder of the First Battle of Ypres. From Zonnebekke, some five miles east-north-east from Ypres itself, the front line ran south for just over four miles before making a right angle back towards Ypres for a further one-and-a-half miles. Trenches hardly existed and barbed wire was barely apparent. Overlooked by German artillery and machine guns, the 7th Division were bombarded continuously by day and night from the heights of the Passchendaele Ridge. On the morning of the 21st, they were hit by shells from 8 in. howitzers, as well as high explosive and shrapnel. Relentless infantry assaults followed. On the left of the line, the German 52nd Reserve Division pressed forward with reckless gallantry. Outnumbering the defenders by about six to one, they advanced, one observer noted, 'singing and waving their rifles in the air'. They paid a heavy price for a display of incredible bravery. They came forward time and time again, and repeatedly, the soldiers of the 7th Division shot them down.

British wounded being evacuated to England. This photograph shows walking wounded going aboard a hospital ship on their way back to Blighty. These are probably casualties from the Battle of the Aisne.

In the centre, successive waves of the 54th Reserve Division and the 3rd Cavalry Division pressed hard against the 2nd Green Howards and 2nd Royal Scots Fusiliers, part of the 21st Brigade. The battalions wavered briefly and some German troops broke through between the two units. They ran into another company of Royal Scots at Polderhoek Château who sent them reeling back with sustained fire. The line reformed and the Germans withdrew, leaving behind a terrible legacy of dead and wounded.

It was at this point that the mistaken withdrawal of the 2nd Cavalry Division from Hollebeke opened a one mile gap in the British line. The 7th Division's commander, Gen. Capper, threw in all the troops he could find to support his right flank which was left exposed because of the cavalry's move. Two companies of the 2nd Scots Guards, the Divisional Cyclists and the Divisional Cavalry, the Northumberland Hussars (who became the first Territorial Force soldiers to see action), went forward, but the Bavarian Cavalry Division failed to take advantage of the error.

Even so, Rawlinson, the IV Corps commander, reacting as best he could in the confusion of lost and delayed messages, of incomplete information and inaccurate assessments, decided to move the 7th Cavalry Brigade on the far left of his line to act as a reserve if the Germans tried to exploit the gap.

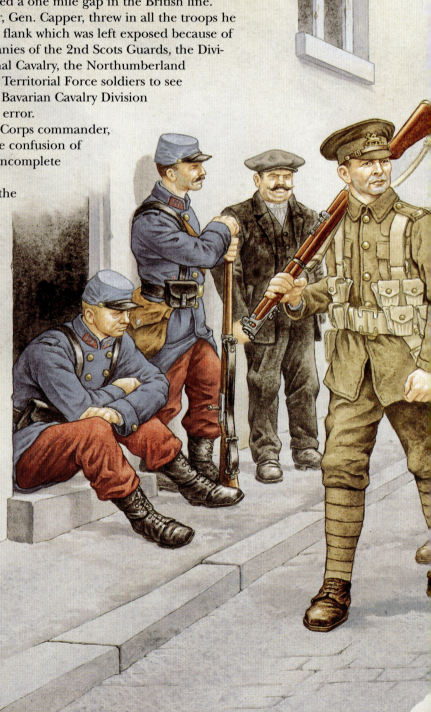

THE 1ST DIVISION ON THE MARCH, 20 OCTOBER 1914
The 1st Division moved out of its billets on the morning of 20 October at 0600. The troops were hampered by heavily congested roads but, by that evening, were in position some two and a half miles to the east of Ypres to the left of IV corps. The advance proper would start the following morning.

The enemy discovered that the withdrawal of the 7th Cavalry Brigade had left a small but vital hole between the left of the 7th Division and the right of I Corps, and the 52nd Reserve Division renewed its attacks. With the support of a devastating barrage, it nearly won the day, getting to within 100 metres of the British line. The gap was hastily plugged by the Irish Guards and disaster averted. The 22nd Brigade remained, though, under persistent and effective artillery attack, and that evening the brigade commander, Gen. Lawford, got permission to shorten his line by withdrawing his left from the Salient and linking up directly with I Corps. For Haig's men, the soldiers of the 1st and 2nd Divisions, 21 October was supposed to be the day on which they would start the march to the German frontier. Haig himself had doubts, but nonetheless planned the advance with his customary attention to detail. The French general, de Mitry, whose Cavalry Corps covered Haig's left flank, was fully briefed about the British plans. With the 2nd Division forward and on the right, the 1st Division behind it and to the left, I Corps moved forward to meet the foe.

They started late. 1st Division was delayed because roads and bridges were crammed with traffic, but initially, the advance went reasonably well. By early afternoon, the 2nd Division was almost alongside the desperately pressed 7th Division. There had been losses from German flanking fire, the 2nd Ox & Bucks Light Infantry taking more than 200 casualties but the artillery enjoyed excellent targets. One battery engaged waves of German infantry in the open and at short range.

By 1400 hours, the leading formations of the 2nd Division were between 200 to 400 metres from the main German defence line. Increasing enemy fire, supported by heavy artillery, persuaded the 2nd Division to dig in and maintain its position. Inevitably, there were some German counterattacks, mounted probably by troops of the 52nd Reserve Division, but they were not pressed with any enthusiasm.

The 1st Division also made steady progress but, by noon, an ominous situation developed. The French cavalry on their left, under attack by the 46th Reserve Division, received orders to retire as more enemy troops seemed to be approaching from the north. To his credit, the French commander refused to expose the British flank without a formal order, and even then many isolated bodies of French soldiers remained in action until dark.

As Haig heard of the French withdrawal, Rawlinson arrived in person to tell him of the heavy attacks upon IV Corps whose Reserve was reduced to a single cavalry brigade. It seemed clear that the Germans were engaged in a strenuous offensive designed to close in on Ypres from the north-east and the south-east.

At 1500 hours, Haig ordered his command to dig in where they were. Both Divisions faced increasing resistance, but they were not totally unsuccessful. The *Official History* made the point succinctly: 'In spite of the numerical superiority, 5 divisions against 2, and the exposed left flank of the I Corps where most of the casualties occurred, the Germans had done little more than bring the British advance to a halt, and that at exceedingly heavy cost.'

ARMENTIÈRES AND LA BASSÉE

In the south, II Corps and III Corps fought on. In the five weeks between 14 October and 22 November, British and Indian casualties were about 27,000 officers and men. Their efforts, nonetheless, would be overshadowed by the struggle for Ypres itself.

The German offensive by the Sixth Army had forced II Corps to conduct a fighting withdrawal to a reserve line that Smith-Dorrien had already earmarked. It was so well chosen that it remained, virtually unchanged, the British front line for the next four years.

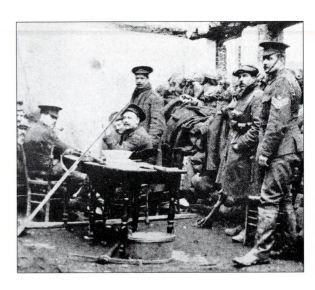

British troops in a barricaded house in the vicinity of Ypres, 1914. The occupants are clearly under no immediate threat and the earth-filled sacks suggest protection against shell splinters rather than firing positions. This could well be a sergeants' mess, the inhabitants wallowing in the sybaritic luxury with which senior NCOs surround themselves whenever possible.

By the evening of 22 October, II Corps were in their new positions. The gap on their left, caused by the retirement of the French cavalry, was filled by the Jullundur Brigade of the Indian Army.

On 26 October, the Germans launched a major assault at Neuve Chapelle – a name which was to feature more prominently in the actions of 1915 – with six infantry regiments, two Jaeger battalions and exceptionally heavy artillery support. In four days of fierce fighting, the Germans suffered about 6,000 casualties and achieved nothing. They actually occupied Neuve Chapelle, but later withdrew, leaving a British patrol to advance cautiously into the ruins in the early morning of 29 October.

The offensive failed and it was not renewed, for the Sixth Army's artillery went north to support the assault on Ypres. The 26th Division which had been the mainstay of the attack also moved north of the River Lys to be flung against the British positions along the Messines-Wytschaete Ridge.

While II Corps was busy at Neuve Chapelle, Pulteney's III Corps, greatly outnumbered, faced an onslaught at Armentières by most of XIII Corps, the 48th Reserve Division, XIX Corps and the I Cavalry Corps. Initially, the attacks appeared less resolute than those against II Corps, even though Armentières was substantially more important.

III Corps still had a hard time of it against a numerically superior enemy with substantial artillery backing. Three BEF battalions, the 1st Leicester, 1st East Yorks and 2nd Durham Light Infantry faced assaults by at least ten German battalions over four days. German dead and wounded piled up before the British positions but it was no bloodless victory. In the 16 days between 15 October and the end of the month, III Corps had casualties of 207 officers and 5,572 men.

By 30 October, attacks in the south were clearly waning. The fighting at Ypres sucked in more and more resources, and not even the mighty German army could attack continually along the entire front. By 2 November, von Falkenhayn had abandoned any thoughts of sustained battle south of the Lys.

Between the 29th and 30th October, II Corps was relieved by the Lahore and Meerut Divisions of the Indian Corps. Smith-Dorrien's men had been in constant action since 23 August. The bone-weary soldiers looked forward to the ten days rest in billets that they had been promised. It was not to be. On 1 November, II Corps began to send battalions north – to Ypres.

Indian Troops on the way to Messines. The Lahore and Meerut Divisions substantially bolstered the BEF and boosted morale despite the fact that the Indian troops suffered cruelly in the cold Flanders weather. Trained essentially for action on the North-West Frontier of India, the Indian Army had been starved of equipment by a parsimonious government. They fought with an intense and rare courage, and Khudadad Khan, a sepoy of the 129th Baluchis, became the first Indian soldier ever to win the Victoria Cross for his outstanding gallantry at the Messines Ridge. Sepoy Khudadad Khan, badly wounded in the action, received his award from King George V personally in December 1914 at an investiture held at the Indian field hospital. He survived the war to return to his village of Chakwal in northern India.

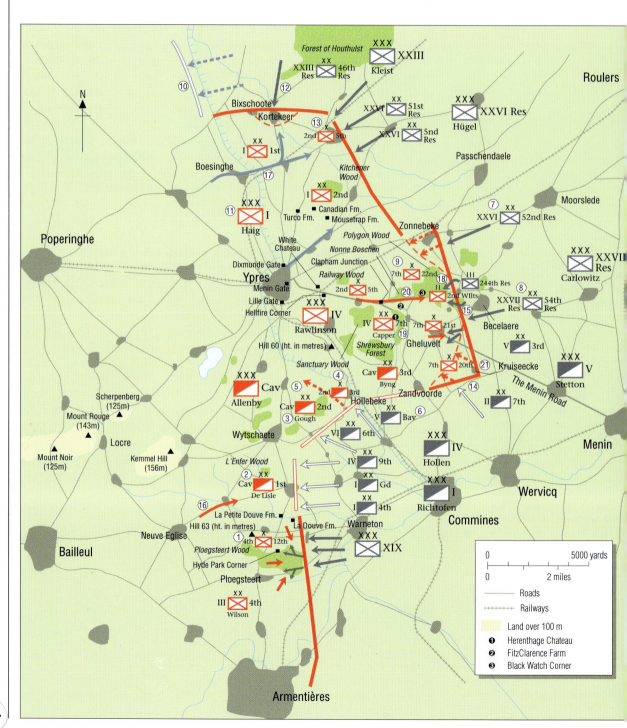

Roulers

Forest of Houthulst

XXX
XXIII
Kleist

XXIII
Res

XX
46th
Res

XXVI
51st
Res

XXX
XXVI Res
Hügel

Bixschoote

Kortekeer

XX
2nd 5th

XXVI
5nd
Res

Passchendaele

I
XX
1st

Boesinghe

Kitchener
Wood

Moorslede

XX
I 2nd

XXVI
52nd Res

Zonnebeke

Canadian Fm.

XXX
I
Haig

Turco Fm.

Mousetrap Fm.

White
Chateau

Polygon Wood

XXX
XXVII
Carlowitz

Poperinghe

Nonne Boschen

Clapham Junction

Dixmunde Gate

Ypres

Railway Wood

XX
7th 22nd

III
244th Res

XX
2nd 5th

XX
7th

XX
XXVII 54th
Res Res

Menin Gate

Lille Gate

Hellfire Corner

XXX
IV
Rawlinson

XX
2nd Wilts

XX
IV 7th
Capper

XX
7th 21st

Becelaere

V
XX
3rd

Hill 60 (ht. in metres)

Gheluvelt

XXX
V
Stetton

Sanctuary Wood

Shrewsbury
Forest

XX
Cav 3rd
Byng

XX
7th 20th

The Menin Road

Kruiseecke

XXX
Cav
Allenby

XX
2nd 3rd

Zandvoorde

II
XX
7th

XX
Cav 2nd
Gough

Hollebeke

V
XX
Bav

Wytschaete

VI
XX
6th

XXX
IV
Hollen

Menin

L'Enfer Wood

IV
XX
9th

XX
Cav 1st
De Lisle

I
XX
Gd

XXX
I
Richtofen

Wervicq

La Petite Douve Fm.

Hill 63 (ht. in metres)

I
XX
4th

Commines

Neuve Eglise

La Douve Fm.

Warneton

XX
4th 12th

XXX
XIX

Bailleul

Ploegsteert Wood

Hyde Park Corner

Ploegsteert

III
XX
4th
Wilson

Armentières

Scherpenberg
(125m)

Mount Rouge
(143m)

Locre

Mount Noir
(125m)

Kemmel Hill
(156m)

N

0		5000 yards
0		2 miles

Roads

Railways

Land over 100 m

❶ Herenthage Chateau
❷ FitzClarence Farm
❸ Black Watch Corner

On the morning of 22 October, the great German offensive to seize Calais began. At the time, it seemed all the effort was concentrated on two sections of the line. Only later was it apparent that the Germans tried to break through along the entire front. Simultaneous attacks were launched, as we have seen, against Armentières and La Bassée, and against the Belgians at the Yser. Falkenhayn was also determined to pierce the French held section between the British and the Belgians.

The German monograph, *Ypres 1914* is less than accurate in describing the situation on 22 October. It says 'a strong position lay to our immediate front. It followed a line Bixschoote-Langemarck-Zonnebeke-Reutel-Gheluvelt, and I and IV British as well as the French IX Corps, all picked troops, had been located there. They had dug a well-planned maze of trenches behind barbed-wire entanglements before a single German shell arrived to disturb their work.'

It was untrue. The French IX Corps only arrived the following afternoon. The 'well-planned maze of trenches' was a hastily-dug selection of holes and unconnected short lengths of trench, barely three feet deep without traverses, supports or dug-outs. There was no wire. The positions had already been bombarded for two days. Neither were the defenders 'picked troops', but ordinary soldiers who happened to be rather good at their job.

Two major attacks took place against the British; one against the 1st & 2nd Divisions around Langemarck, the other on the 7th Division.

On the northern face of the salient, near Bixschoote, after a relatively quiet morning, a fierce German attack developed against I Corps positions. It was largely unsuccessful except in the centre at Kortekeer. There, the 1st Cameron Highlanders, without artillery support and with a 400 yard gap between themselves and the 1st Coldstream on their right, were outflanked because their defensive line was no more than a series of unconnected positions. As the light faded, the Camerons were picked off by German troops in the gap between the Scots and the Coldstream. The Highlanders retreated, reluctantly abandoning Kortekeer to a triumphant enemy.

PUTTYING-UP

The line stabilised and Haig considered a counterattack. He pulled the 2nd King's Royal Rifle Corps from corps reserve and the 1st Queen's from 3rd Brigade, took the 2nd South Staffs from the 6th Brigade and the 1st Loyal North Lancashire from 2nd Brigade. It was the first step in a process known as 'putting-up'. Haig abandoned a formal Order of Battle, instead shifting infantry, artillery, cavalry and even engineer units, irrespective of origin, to the most critical points. Whenever the enemy explored a weak spot, Haig moved his 'Fire Brigade' to bolster the defence.

It was brilliant improvisation and a major factor in the successful defence at Ypres. Mons and Le Cateau were triumphs for Smith-Dorrien, First Ypres stands as a tribute to Haig's substantial military skills.

The 5th Infantry Brigade, part of the 2nd Division of I Corps, were attacked by XXVI Reserve Corps and a division of the XXIII Reserve Corps. Under artillery bombardment for much of the day, as well as incessant small arms fire, the 2nd Worcestershire, 2nd Ox & Bucks Light

55

Infantry and 2nd Highland Light Infantry were finally attacked by German infantry at dusk. The dark mass of Germans was met by solid and sustained fire. The British heard the Germans gathering their casualties long into the night.

The 7th Division, severely bombarded along their whole front from 0700, also inflicted profound damage upon its attackers. A German wireless message ordering 'a vigorous attack on the left of the Becelaere-Zandvoorde position' was intercepted. Haig moved his reserves to counter this threat from the 3rd, the 7th, and Bavarian Cavalry Divisions, supported by 4, 9, & 10 Jaeger Battalions. The attack was far from 'vigorous'. *Ypres 1914* claimed that it 'could not be carried out . . because of the strong hostile position, which had good dugouts, without support of heavy artillery'.

Instead, the 21st Infantry Brigade at Reutel on the eastern face of the salient faced a massive and determined thrust by the German 54th

Soldiers of General Duke Albrecht's Fourth Army manning a machine gun position alongside a Belgian road. Although is it clearly a posed photograph, this is a real defensive position, designed to operate against a real enemy.

Reserve Division. The 2nd Green Howards, the 2nd Wiltshire and the 2nd Royal Scots Fusiliers, supported by 28 18-pdrs. and four 60-pdr. guns, winnowed the enemy ranks. Caught in the open, the luckless volunteers wilted. No soldiers could have continued. The survivors fell back leaving their dead and wounded, according to one British war diary, 'piled in heaps'.

By nightfall on the 22nd, the soldiers of three British infantry divisions, the 1st, 2nd & 7th, and the 3rd Cavalry Division faced six German infantry divisions and three of cavalry. However, reinforcements were reaching both the French and the Belgians, and the first Indian troops from the Lahore Division arrived to support the Cavalry Corps at Messines and Wulverghem.

ALLIED COUNTERATTACK

The arrival of the French IX Corps sparked Foch into enthusiastic action. He immediately ordered a general offensive along the French line. He also wanted to relieve pressure on the British and he asked Sir John French to help by instructing the whole BEF to attack the next morning.

Haig received the orders shortly before 0200 on 23 October. They required a general assault to be launched at 0900. To arrange this along a 15 mile front at seven hours' notice would be difficult with modern communications. In 1914, it was wishful thinking.

The French offensive quickly came to a halt, but there were positive results. The French IX Corps took over the whole BEF sector from Bixschoote to Zonnebeke. This allowed 1st Division to become part of I Corps reserve, and 2nd Division to close up alongside the hard-pressed 7th Division south of Zonnebeke.

On the same day there was also a successful counterattack against Kortekeer. Brig.Gen. Bulfin sent in five battalions with artillery support. They released 54 Cameron Highlanders held by the enemy and took 350 prisoners of their own from the 209th, 210th and 211th Reserve Infantry Regiments.

A mixture of civilians and French troops watch Spahis escorting German prisoners to the rear. Both the British and French popular press tended to stress the ferocity of colonial troops and their alleged predilection for beheading the enemy. Not surprisingly, German papers were equally quick to condemn what they saw as a breach of civilised warfare – a quaint conceit in a conflict which saw, among other things, the use of choking and blistering chemical agents on a large scale, the introduction of unrestricted submarine attacks and the execution of civilians.

The I Corps front each side of Kortekeer, however, was already under pressure. One attack, led by mounted officers, was repulsed by a half company of the 1st Gloucesters. Others followed, both on the Gloucesters and on the 1st Coldstream on the left and the 2nd Welch on their right. In some spots, the Germans got within 50 yards before succumbing to a withering fire. At the end of the day, the Gloucesters had fired an average of 500 rounds per man and the ground was strewn with German casualties.

The Germans counterattacked near Kortekeer as dusk fell. They were beaten off, but Bulfin decided to retreat to his previous line. Apart from increasing British confidence and providing some interesting souvenirs, the operation had cost 1st Division 1,344 casualties.

Their opponents had also had a gruelling time. *Ypres 1914*, summarises: 'With the failure of the 46th Reserve Division to gain a decisive victory between Bixschoote and Langemarck on the 22nd and 23rd October, the fate of the XXVI and XXVIII Reserve Corps was also settled.

THE 7th DIVISION FALLING BACK (2 BN., ROYAL SCOTS FUSILIERS, 21st BDE.) 25–26 OCTOBER 1914 During the fighting of the 22 to 24 October the 7th Division had lost over 120 officers and 2,700 men injured or killed. A series of further assaults on the 25 and 36 October drove the division further back from the village of Kruiseecke, and it was in danger of breaking altogether. However, although they were driven back over three miles, the line held.

For the time being, any further thought of a breakthrough was out of the question. They had suffered heavily in the contest against a war-experienced and numerically superior opponent entrenched in strongly fortified positions.' Throughout the night of 23 October, the 7th Division line was subjected to persistent rifle fire and attempted infiltration. As dawn approached on the 24th, the full length of the position was extensively bombarded. From Zandvoorde to Kruiseecke, northwards via Poezelhoek and Reutel, just in front of Polygon Wood, to Zonnebeke where the Division maintained contact with the French, the hostile barrage smashed into the 7th Division.

A heavy infantry assault followed. The 243rd, 244th, 246th and 247th Regiments of the 53rd and 54th Reserve Divisions of the XXVII Reserve Corps made three attacks. All three failed, except at Reutel where the 2nd Wiltshires held the left of the 21st Brigade's line at its junction with the 22nd Brigade. The area had been heavily shelled and attacked the

German troops bivouac in a Belgian farmyard. This photograph probably pre-dates the Ypres battle, but nonetheless gives an excellent impression of the German soldier.

previous day. Some British troops had pulled back in the fighting and the Wiltshires simply did not know that their flanks were unguarded. Three battalions of the 244th Reserve Infantry Regiment overwhelmed the Wiltshires from all sides. At this moment, mid-morning on 24 October, success was clearly within the German grasp. There were no reserves behind the Wiltshires. The way to Ypres was clear. A single, determined thrust would be enough.

Maj.Gen. Capper, commanding the 7th Division, heard of the disaster – that the line had gone and the enemy was breaking through into Polygon Wood – and sent the Northumberland Hussars to check the enemy progress. In the interim, he assembled any soldiers he could find into a blocking force. Staff officers, clerks, cooks – one of whom was armed only with a ladle – and orderlies became infantry sections. Capper also asked Haig for help.

In fierce fighting, the Northumberland Hussars, with the 2nd Warwicks, efficiently checked the enemy advance. The Hussars escaped lightly, but the Warwicks' 300 casualties included the death of their CO. Haig sent the 5th Brigade, and the French 6th Cavalry Division provided a regiment in support.

The Germans made little attempt to exploit their success. Having taken their objective, the German soldiers stood or sat about, uncertain of their next move. Lack of training was to blame. In their turn, the enemy would watch British soldiers behave the same way at Loos, Suvla Bay and the Somme.

Reutel, separated from Polygon Wood by a small valley, remained in German hands. On the right of the 7th Division, the Germans launched a heavy attack during the afternoon. Accompanied by violent shelling, they exerted enormous pressure on the British line, but it managed to hold. The Germans launched a further attack towards the evening with the same result.

THE 7TH DIVISION ON THE MENIN ROAD

The 7th Division was showing signs of exhaustion. In the fighting of the 22–24 October, the Division had lost 120 officers and 2,700 men. The 2nd Wiltshires had virtually ceased to exist; three battalions, the Scots Guards, Royal Welch Fusiliers and the South Staffordshires, had each lost more than 500 officers and men, and three others – the Grenadier Guards, the Queen's and the Warwicks – more than 300. Overall, the Division's total casualties amounted to 45 per cent of its officers and 37 per cent of the men.

A series of assaults on the 7th Division on the 25th and 26th October finally drove them from Kruiseecke, a hamlet south of the Menin Road. During 36 hours of bombardment, mostly by heavy guns firing 210 cm shells, men were buried alive in the sandy soil, only to be dug-out by their comrades and to resume their place in the firing line to meet yet another infantry attack. Eventually, part of the 7th Division gave way on the afternoon of the 26th.

They had endured a night of torrential rain and consistent attacks, with only a two hour respite before dawn. Then the shelling began once more. In the middle of the morning, three dismounted cavalry regiments, including the 23rd Dragoons, and an infantry regiment, assaulted the drenched and muddy British. This attack was beaten back, but a few small groups of Germans slipped between the disconnected British positions. The bombardment continued and there was an ominous trickle of men to the rear: men who were wounded; men who had been blown out of their trenches; men looking for the remains of their units; men whose rifles no longer worked because of the sand clogging the mechanism; men exhausted and shocked by nights and days of fighting.

In early afternoon, a fresh, massive enemy assault began. The German soldiers who had penetrated the line earlier in the day shouted 'Retire! Retire!' as their own men got closer. More shells rained down. Without thinking, fearful of being cut off, some troops fell back. A hasty scramble became a near rout as the charge pressed home. The defence fragmented over a distance of three miles but the enemy could not take

Casualty evacuation. From the very earliest days of the war, British casualty evacuation was handled efficiently – the lessons of South Africa had been thoroughly absorbed. By the time of La Bassée and First Ypres, each division had two general and two stationary hospitals. The general hospitals had 520 beds, the stationary 200 beds. Further, each division had a clearing hospital located close to its operational area. By 11 October, eight ambulance trains were operating from the clearing hospitals as well as motor ambulances. Closer to the front line, advanced dressing stations took immediate care of the wounded sent on from regimental aid posts. Horse ambulances, similar to the one in this picture, were used as well as motor vehicles.

① **27 October** Army Group Fabeck formed out of II Bavarian Corps, XV Corps, 6th Reserve Division and the 48th Reserve Division

② **29 October** 54th Reserve Division attacks the Scots Guards at Becelaere

③ **29 October** 16th Reserve Division breaks through British lines towards Gheluvelt, 7th Division are forced back from their position in bitter fighting

④ **29 October** The 1st Grenadier Guards manage to hold their positions in a series of savage engagements, by nightfall the line was rejoined, however the cross-roads to the north remained in Bavarian hands

⑤ **29 October** French IX Corps, supported by 6th Brigade of Haig's 2nd Division, advance more than a mile, recapturing Zonnebeke, Bixschoote and Kortekeer.

⑥ **30 October** At Zonnebeke, diversionary attacks launched by the inexperienced XXVII Reserve Corps are beaten back with heavy losses

⑦ **30 October** The advance by the German 54th Reserve Division and the 30th Division is halted at Gheluvelt

⑧ **30 October** The 39th Division takes the hillock of Zandvoorde after and intense artillery bombardment, 7th Cavalry Brigade is driven back towards their reserve lines

⑨ **30 October** Haig requests immediate help from the French IX Corps, Dubois immediately sends a Brigade of Cuirassiers to his aid

⑩ **30 October** The 3rd and 4th Bavarian Divisions attack the Comines Canal in the direction of Hollebeke, they succeed in driving back the 3rd Cavalry Division

⑪ **31 October** The 54th Reserve Division, 30th Division and the 16th Bavarian Reserve Regiment advance towards Gheluvelt, and, after heavy fighting, they capture it

⑫ **31 October** The 2nd Worcesters attack against the odds and manage to recapture the Château of Gheluvelt

⑬ **2 November** After four days during which it had changed hands a number of times, Army group Fabeck gains control of the Messines ridge and a grand attack is planned for the tenth

⑭ **10 November** The 7th Division and the 3rd Infantry Brigade are withdrawn from the line having sustained heavy losses in the course of the battle so far

⑮ **11 November** The Bavarian 4th Division attacks the newly arrived II Corps south of the Menin road, the Germans fall back under heavy fire.

⑯ **11 November** The 2nd and 4th Guard Brigades of Army Group Linsingen advance along the Menin road towards the position of the 1st Division

⑰ **11 November** Men of the 1st Foot Guards break through the British lines, but under heavy fire they lose their cohesion and take cover in Nonneboschen (Nun's Wood)

⑱ **11 November** The 2nd Oxfordshire and Buckinghamshire Light Infantry attack Nonnesboschen, clearing the Guard from the wood. This proves to be the last major engagement of First Ypres

advantage. Clusters of stubborn men in khaki stopped, regrouped, and kept on firing. The meagre reserves came up and a new line formed.

The survivors reassembled, even though many men had lost their officers and their battalion headquarters. They formed sections, platoons, companies under lance-corporals, corporals and sergeants before the bonus of the arrival of precious replacements. 1,000 men, some recovered from wounds, others rejoined Reservists and a sprinkling of officers, some newly commissioned from Sandhurst, arrived and the 7th Division was back in action the next morning – now directly under Haig, as Rawlinson had gone back to Britain to organise the new 8th Division.

On the rest of the front and on the southern battlefields of La Bassée and Armentières, there was less action. Although the German attacks had diminished, neither the French nor the British could seize the initiative and advance. Indeed, Sir John French warned Kitchener that unless the supply of ammunition could be maintained, his troops would soon be without artillery support. He was told to economise.

French continued to send wildly optimistic reports to the War Office: on 24 October, the battle was 'practically won'; on the 25th, the situation was 'more favourable every hour', and the 26th showed that the enemy was 'quite incapable of making any strong and sustained attack'. By the 27th 'it was only necessary to press the enemy hard to ensure complete success and victory'.

GERMAN PLANS, 27-31 OCTOBER

Falkenhayn thought otherwise. On 27 October, he visited Crown Prince Rupprecht's headquarters to review progress. His assessment was blunt. The Fourth and Sixth Armies had clearly failed, despite their superiority in numbers. Worse, the French had reinforced their line and even attacked towards the Ypres ridge. The only consolation was that the French had drawn reinforcements from other fronts. What they could do, Falkenhayn could do better.

Accordingly, he decided that a new formation would join the German Order of Battle, Army Group Fabeck. This would be formed from two regular corps moved from France, the II Bavarian and the XV Corps; the 26th Division, already serving with Fabeck's XIII Corps, would be relieved by the 48th Reserve Division from Metz and be added to the total together with the 6th Bavarian Reserve Division from Fourth Army.

THE BATTLE FOR YPRES

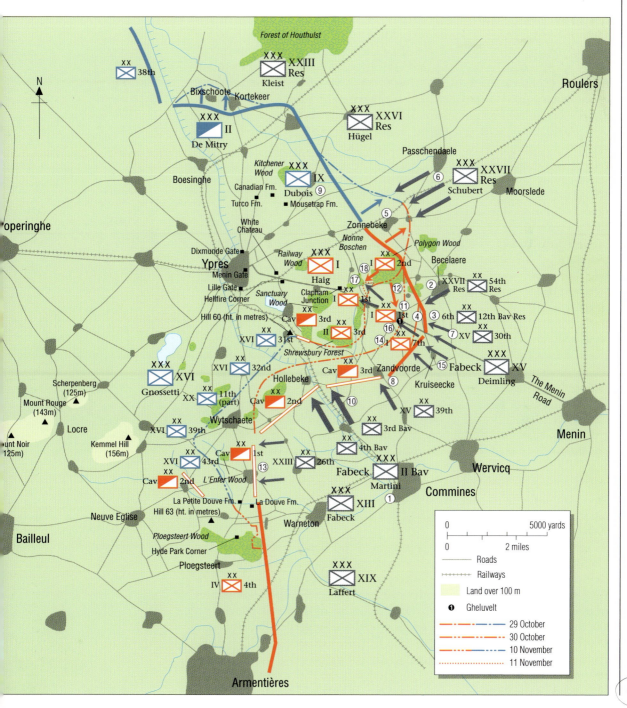

Fabeck would thus command five regular divisions, and one of recently recruited volunteers, who would make up for their inexperience by their enthusiasm. To this formidable force was added even more artillery – a total of 262 heavy guns and 484 smaller calibre pieces.

Although Army Group Fabeck formed a new right wing of the Sixth Army, Falkenhayn emphasised that it had one single purpose. It was to strike a massive blow where the enemy was weakest and the line of approach most direct – against the British from Ploegsteert Wood to Gheluvelt. Breaking the line anywhere along this six-mile sector would lead to the capture of the higher ground, particularly the Messines Ridge. From there the enemy's positions could be comprehensively enfiladed.

The troops must not be used elsewhere without the permission of Supreme Headquarters. The great assault was timed for 30th October. Fourth and Sixth Army would attack on their fronts to prevent the movement of Allied reserves. To cover the concentration of Army Group Fabeck, it was decided to capture Gheluvelt the day before the big attack.

Fourth Army sent a wireless message to XXVII Reserve Corps ordering co-operation with the 6th Bavarian Reserve Division in the assault on Gheluvelt to be launched at 0530 hours on 29 October. The message was intercepted and the information reached Haig during the afternoon of the 28th. Given precedence over other messages, the information did not get to the battalions until midnight, even though most of them were a mere 3,000 yards from I Corps Headquarters. This was not inefficiency – Haig probably had the best staff in the BEF – but a problem of communications. There was no wireless equipment; telephone cables were broken time and time again by shelling; runners were cut down by rifle and artillery fire.

THE BATTLE FOR GHELUVELT

At 0500 hours, Haig's men were ready for the anticipated German attack. It was dark and foggy, with a smell of damp earth and damp clothing. The fog isolated sections and platoons from one another. It was generally believed that the German offensive would be against the junction of the 7th and the 1st Divisions at the cross-roads one mile south-east of Gheluvelt.

Fabeck confounded the general opinion. At Becelaere, a mile north of Gheluvelt, a regiment of the 54th Reserve Division attacked the 1st Scots Guards with no preliminary bombardment. They advanced in a dense mass, one battalion each side of the road and one in the rear on it. It was only when a gust of wind temporarily cleared the mist that the Guards saw the enemy approaching at a fast pace a mere 80 yards away. A desperate defence began.

Immediately to the right, a company of the Black Watch and some Coldstream Guards under the command of Capt. J.E. Gibbs faced a very determined attack which was pushed home with great resolution. On their right, separated by a considerable gap, two diminished companies of the 1st Coldstream, a much reduced company of the Black Watch and the machine gun section of 1st Gloucesters confronted three battalions of the 16th Bavarian Reserve Infantry. They advanced with reckless courage, gaining ground as the British struggled with faulty ammunition. Two British machine guns jammed and the rifle fire was seriously disrupted. Some cartridges were too large; others had too thin a casing

By the end of 1914, there were six general hospitals at Le Havre where this photograph of drivers belonging to one of the Motor Ambulance Convoys were photographed reading, presumably, about the war. The popular British press commanded a ready sale among the troops and, later in the war, a number of soldiers expressed astonishment at the activities of small French paper boys who infiltrated the trench system in order to hawk their wares – the Daily Mail is invariably mentioned as the paper which the enterprising children were selling.

and the bolt could only be opened by lowering the butt to the thigh and tugging or, in the worst cases, kicking with a hefty boot.

In the fog, and the sporadic fire, some Bavarians broke into the British positions after only 20 minutes. Collecting more men, they began a flank attack northwards, rolling up the Black Watch and the Coldstream Guards very quickly. The British had no artillery support: the gunners were limited to nine rounds per day and were instructed to use it only against the enemy's guns.

Moving on, the Bavarians fired on Gibbs and his men. Gibbs reorganised his defences to deal with this new threat as well as the assault on his front, and sent runners to Brigade Headquarters at Gheluvelt and to the Scots Guards to his north asking for aid. After he passed into the smoke of bursting shells, the runner to Brigade was never seen again, but Fitzclarence, commanding the 1st (Guards) Brigade, learned of the disaster from a wounded officer at 0700. He immediately sent 1st Gloucesters to the rescue. 'D' Company of the 1st Gloucesters had already moved off on the initiative of the CO, Lt.Col. A. C. Lovett. The others followed. One company was heavily shelled and split up, another lost its way in the fog and joined up with the 1st Scots Guards. 'D' Company itself came under attack on the main road and the fourth later joined it, its soldiers getting into the firing line wherever they could.

Gibbs' command came under renewed shelling at about 1000. More German infantry were flung into the attack and the British defence was finally eliminated. On the left, the 1st Scots Guards clung on tenaciously, receiving piecemeal reinforcements throughout the day.

A rare, possibly unique, snapshot of a German first aid post on the Ypres sector during the fighting in the Autumn of 1914. The post is close to the front line and the primitive conditions under which the medical staff of both sides worked are apparent.

Haig's 'puttying-up' was now in full swing, troops being committed irrespective of brigade. Slowly, bitterly, grimly, lost ground was recovered. The Bavarians were forced back in a deadly contest which prevented the envelopment of the whole British position. South of the Menin Road, the 7th Division had also begun the day in readiness. Shouting and firing filtered through the fog but they were cheerfully unaware that the enemy had taken the cross-roads a mere 200 metres away. Manning the British positions at this point were the 1st Grenadier Guards, the 2nd Scots Guards and the 2nd Border Regiment. At 0700, just as the Grenadiers were thinking it was all a false alarm and the other two battalions had moved towards the rear to eat and rest, German troops to the south attacked the 2nd Royal Scots Fusiliers.

By 0730, German heavy guns were raining shells on the Grenadiers. After 30 minutes, four battalions of German troops launched themselves at the heavily outnumbered Guardsmen. In bitter fighting, the Grenadiers slowly gave ground, the struggle becoming increasingly barbaric. 'Some was strangling the Boche,' one participant recalled, 'some was stabbing them as they come at us, we just did what we could.' All along the line, British units became inextricably tangled as the fighting raged. When darkness came and heavy rain began to fall, all assaults had been beaten off, all of the lost ground reclaimed and the line rejoined – but it was south of the cross-roads, which remained in Bavarian hands.

Losses were high. The 1st Scots Guards casualties were eight officers and 336 men; the Black Watch lost five officers and 250 men. Descriptions like company, battalion and brigade now become increasingly meaningless when describing British units – by 1 November, for example, the *battalion* of the 1st Loyal North Lancs consisted of one officer and 35 men.

French Cuirassiers leave for the north. This photograph gives an excellent impression of how much space cavalry actually occupied – the photograph shows only about 50 men and their horses – a single regiment would take up about a kilometre while on the march.

Elsewhere, there seemed to be less cause for concern. Sir John French and Foch continued their offensive blithely unaware of Army Group Fabeck. The French IX Corps advanced more than a mile, recapturing Zonnebeke, Bixschoote and Kortekeer and penetrating the Passchendaele Ridge. The 6th Infantry Brigade of Haig's 2nd Division pushed forward in concert with the French and captured Broodseinde, a mile to the north-east of Zonnebeke. The Cavalry Corps on the Messines-Wyschaete Ridge enjoyed a quiet day, undisturbed as Fabeck's troops moved into position ready for the morning.

Haig returned to his headquarters. Previously at Hooge Château, I Corps had moved that day to the White Château, just east of Ypres, at what became known as Hellfire Corner. The Hooge Château had housed both I Corps and 2nd Division HQ until Haig learned that the 1st Division Commander, Maj.Gen. Lomax and his staff were working in cramped and difficult conditions nearby and living in a two-roomed cottage. Haig, with typical consideration, gave up his own accommodation to help them.

GHQ orders that evening instructed I Corps to continue to co-operate with the French advance. Haig, reviewing accounts of the day's actions and learning that the German artillery had been registering many targets with heavy guns, decided that orders for an offensive could wait until the situation was clearer. He instructed his troops to entrench. A supply of precious barbed wire had been received and some units had the luxury of spreading strands in front of their wet and muddy firing pits.

At Fabeck's headquarters, an Order of the Day was circulating, a stern reminder of the purpose of the imminent battle. 'The break-through will be of decisive importance. We must and will conquer; settle for ever the centuries-long struggle, end the war, and strike the decisive blow against our most detested enemy. We will finish with the British, Indians, Canadians, Moroccans and other trash, feeble adversaries, who surrender in great numbers if they are attacked with vigour.'

Fabeck's offensive was planned to explode all along the line, with the main effort against the British south-east of Ypres. The first targets were Zandvoorde and the Messines Ridge with the object of breaking through

The BEF, in common with its contemporaries, had its complement of cyclists. Classified as mounted troops, they were expected to supplement the traditional cavalry role of scouting. In this photograph, allegedly taken on active service in Flanders but almost certainly posed at an English roadside, cyclists keep a lookout for the enemy. In practice, it soon became apparent that the bicycle was of little use in trench warfare, although its use as a means of personal transport was undeniable and access to a service bicycle was much coveted by men at bases behind the lines.

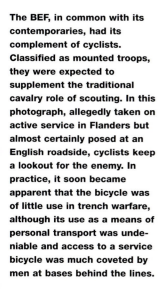

to Kemmel to outflank the Allied line. This would force French, British and Belgians into pell-mell retreat. An important diversionary attack by XXVII Reserve Corps against the French and British line at Zonnebeke would draw in Allied reserves and prevent them being used elsewhere. At dawn, Fabeck's artillery crashed into action.

The diversion failed. Seven *Landwehr* battalions displayed almost unbelievable gallantry until the attack at Zonnebeke finally stuttered to a halt by 0900. Simply, there were no longer enough troops to form an attack line. The dead and wounded were a carpet in front of the British and French who had no difficulty in meeting the assault and needed no reinforcements.

At Gheluvelt, the 54th Reserve Division and the 30th Division attacked along the north of the main road in full daylight. They were in sight for 500 yards as they advanced and only a few survivors reached a position 200 yards from the British line. A second attempt an hour later met the same fate.

On the British right, where the Germans had a superiority of about six to one, at Ploegsteert Wood, Saint Yves, the Messines Ridge and Zandvoorde, the heavy bombardment took its toll. The 7th Cavalry Brigade, with the 22nd Infantry Brigade immediately on their right, were the main victims of concerted shelling. Two squadrons each of the 1st & 2nd Life Guards, and the machine gun sections of the Royal Horse Guards, holding the hillock at Zandvoorde, were blasted from their trenches and attacked by two regiments of the 39th Division and three Jaeger Battalions, who swarmed towards the dazed survivors as the bombardment ceased at about 0800. Two squadrons, together with the RHG machine gunners were cut off and annihilated, only a few men being taken prisoner. Zandvoorde fell. The Germans advanced with great caution, apparently suspecting a trap, and did not occupy the village until 1000 hours. The remains of the 7th Cavalry Brigade retired to their support lines behind Zandvoorde. The 22nd Infantry Brigade were now outflanked and under heavy fire. The first to suffer were the 1st Royal Welch Fusiliers. One Jaeger battalion worked round their open flank to within 30 yards of them; a German field battery, firing shrapnel, added its weight to the fray and within 20 minutes, 276 officers and men were killed. The Jaegers took prisoner the 54 still remaining. None was unwounded.

The 2nd Royal Scots Fusiliers were next but they managed to place eight men across their exposed right flank who dealt with the enemy infantry but were of little use against the 39th Division artillery.

Haig, learning that his right was crumbling and aware of the considerable weight of the enemy facing him, now had the problem of containing and blunting Army Group Fabeck's onslaught. The German attack would shortly threaten the Comines Canal and Hollebeke, whose château was in British hands. Haig ordered the line from Gheluvelt to the bend in the canal north of Hollebeke to be held at all costs. He further decided on a counterattack to retake Zandvoorde and restore the British line. There were few enough troops to hand, so he asked

La Paix, nous la voulons, mais solide et durable
Pour que la Guerre enfin ne soit plus qu'une fable...

If the British soldiers ever believed that they alone were fighting at Ypres, this postcard would have been a cause for instant mayhem. Produced as the BEF moved north into Belgium in October 1914, it shows a French, Belgian and two Russian soldiers posing in front of the Goddess of Victory who is, of course, wearing a tricolour sash against a background of the appropriate national flags.

Dubois, commanding the French IX Corps for help. Without hesitation, that clear-sighted officer handed over a brigade of cuirassiers. Later Dubois' reserve of three infantry battalions together with some artillery was similarly provided without query.

The attempt to recover Zandvoorde temporarily disconcerted the Bavarians who were worried about advancing into a trap where they would meet large numbers of fresh troops. Although Zanvoorde was not recaptured, the German advance stalled.

Even so, the 1st Royal Scots Fusiliers and their neighbours, the Green Howards were dangerously exposed. At 1245, the Fusiliers received orders to withdraw; the same orders did not reach the Green Howards until 1530 – the first messenger was killed on the way. Only 'D' Company and the battalion headquarters of the Scots retired safely. The other three companies attracted a hail of shrapnel whenever they attempted to move. They stayed and fought on. When darkness fell, 130 Royal Scots Fusiliers retired in good order to a new defensive line. Their resistance helped the Green Howards to slip away under cover of hedges and woods, losing only 10 men in the process.

The Comines Canal position, held by six seriously weakened cavalry regiments, was attacked at 1030. The 3rd and 4th Bavarian Divisions struck on either side, thrusting towards Hollebeke. The German infantry made little progress until their artillery literally blew the defenders from their miserable trenches.

The 3rd Cavalry Division wheeled back on its northern flank, abandoning first Hollebeke and then the château. By evening, the British cavalry lay along the 50 metre contour line of the Messines-Wytschaete Ridge.

Rupprecht was 'profoundly disappointed' by the day's events. A great many men had been lost but the British line, although pushed back some three kilometres, was unbroken. Fabeck explained that a fresh assault would be launched against the Messines Ridge that very night. There would be no respite. The offensive would be pressed with even greater vigour.

Fabeck intended to crush the whole of the south of the salient with a simultaneous and decisive breakthrough at Messines and Gheluvelt. An overwhelming victory was essential. The Kaiser himself was visiting the front on the 31st and a triumphal entry into Ypres would be a fitting way to mark the occasion.

Haig had just 21 defiant battalions in his line; battered, reduced in numbers, weary and haggard, but still truculent they faced a massive imbalance of numbers. Despite this, Haig decided to try to regain Zandvoorde and Hollebeke with a composite force, including five battalions of French infantry. This was infinitely preferable to leaving his men on top of the ridge to be shot at whenever the Germans felt like it.

But Fabeck struck first.

22 Battalions of Territorial Force infantry went to the Western Front in 1914 in addition to Yeomanry and Engineer formations. Others went to Gibraltar, Malta, Egypt and India to relieve regular army units. The first non-regular unit to see action was the Northumberland Hussars; the first Territorial infantry to experience combat was the London Scottish at Wytschaete on the Messines Ridge. Seen here are some of the survivors of the action.

DEFENCE OF GHELUVELT
31st October 1914

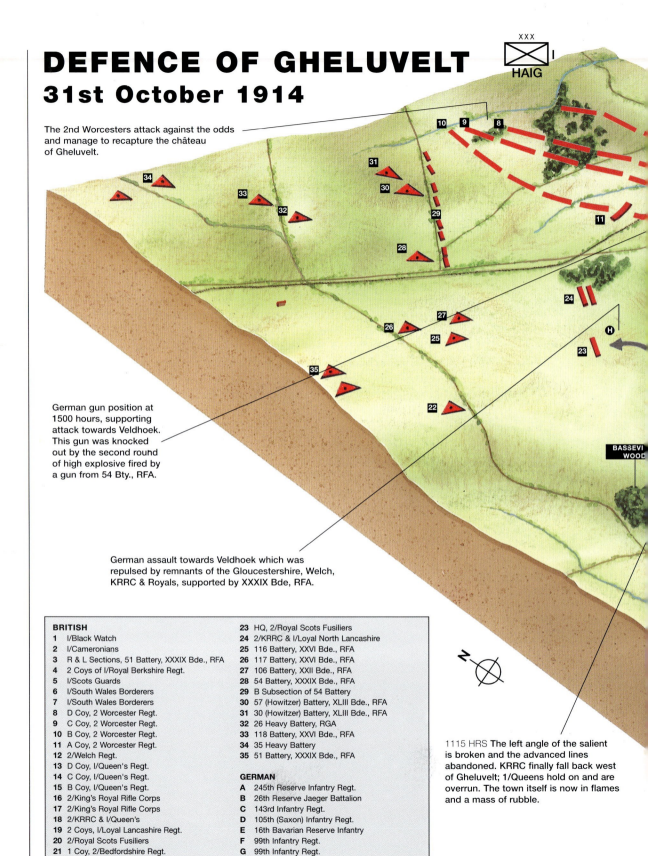

The 2nd Worcesters attack against the odds and manage to recapture the château of Gheluvelt.

German gun position at 1500 hours, supporting attack towards Veldhoek. This gun was knocked out by the second round of high explosive fired by a gun from 54 Bty., RFA.

German assault towards Veldhoek which was repulsed by remnants of the Gloucestershire, Welch, KRRC & Royals, supported by XXXIX Bde, RFA.

XXX
HAIG

BASSEVI
WOOD

N

1115 HRS The left angle of the salient is broken and the advanced lines abandoned. KRRC finally fall back west of Gheluvelt; 1/Queens hold on and are overrun. The town itself is now in flames and a mass of rubble.

BRITISH
1   I/Black Watch
2   I/Cameronians
3   R & L Sections, 51 Battery, XXXIX Bde., RFA
4   2 Coys of I/Royal Berkshire Regt.
5   I/Scots Guards
6   I/South Wales Borderers
7   I/South Wales Borderers
8   D Coy, 2 Worcester Regt.
9   C Coy, 2 Worcester Regt.
10 B Coy, 2 Worcester Regt.
11 A Coy, 2 Worcester Regt.
12 2/Welch Regt.
13 D Coy, I/Queen's Regt.
14 C Coy, I/Queen's Regt.
15 B Coy, I/Queen's Regt.
16 2/King's Royal Rifle Corps
17 2/King's Royal Rifle Corps
18 2/KRRC & I/Queen's
19 2 Coys, I/Loyal Lancashire Regt.
20 2/Royal Scots Fusiliers
21 1 Coy, 2/Bedfordshire Regt.
22 26 Heavy Battery, Royal Garrison Artillery

23 HQ, 2/Royal Scots Fusiliers
24 2/KRRC & I/Loyal North Lancashire
25 116 Battery, XXVI Bde., RFA
26 117 Battery, XXVI Bde., RFA
27 106 Battery, XXII Bde., RFA
28 54 Battery, XXXIX Bde., RFA
29 B Subsection of 54 Battery
30 57 (Howitzer) Battery, XLIII Bde., RFA
31 30 (Howitzer) Battery, XLIII Bde., RFA
32 26 Heavy Battery, RGA
33 118 Battery, XXVI Bde., RFA
34 35 Heavy Battery
35 51 Battery, XXXIX Bde., RFA

GERMAN
A   245th Reserve Infantry Regt.
B   26th Reserve Jaeger Battalion
C   143rd Infantry Regt.
D   105th (Saxon) Infantry Regt.
E   16th Bavarian Reserve Infantry
F   99th Infantry Regt.
G   99th Infantry Regt.

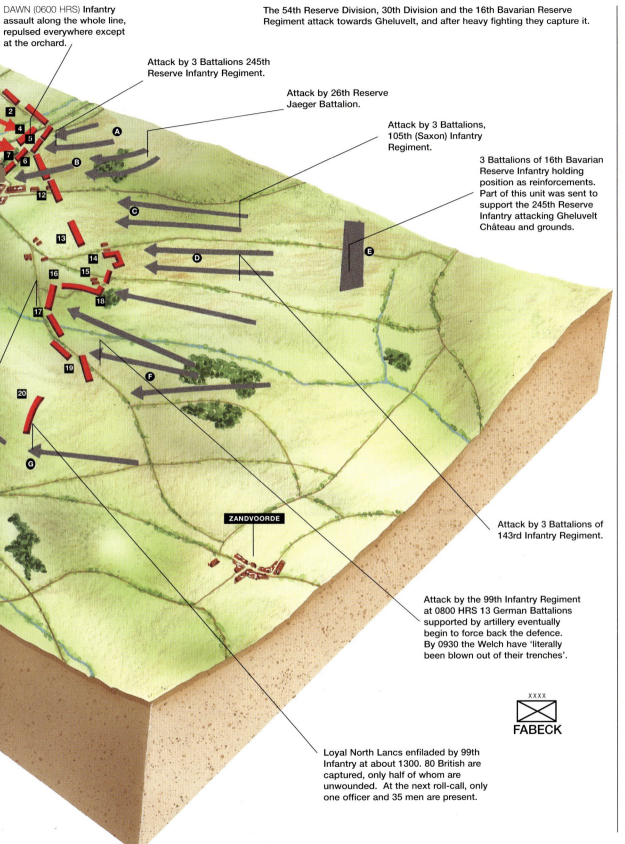

DAWN (0600 HRS) Infantry assault along the whole line, repulsed everywhere except at the orchard.

The 54th Reserve Division, 30th Division and the 16th Bavarian Reserve Regiment attack towards Gheluvelt, and after heavy fighting they capture it.

Attack by 3 Battalions 245th Reserve Infantry Regiment.

Attack by 26th Reserve Jaeger Battalion.

Attack by 3 Battalions, 105th (Saxon) Infantry Regiment.

3 Battalions of 16th Bavarian Reserve Infantry holding position as reinforcements. Part of this unit was sent to support the 245th Reserve Infantry attacking Gheluvelt Château and grounds.

Attack by 3 Battalions of 143rd Infantry Regiment.

Attack by the 99th Infantry Regiment at 0800 HRS 13 German Battalions supported by artillery eventually begin to force back the defence. By 0930 the Welch have 'literally been blown out of their trenches'.

ZANDVOORDE

Loyal North Lancs enfiladed by 99th Infantry at about 1300. 80 British are captured, only half of whom are unwounded. At the next roll-call, only one officer and 35 men are present.

XXXX
FABECK

THE FINALE

In the thin mist of dawn on 31 October 1914, the 16th Bavarian and the 246th Infantry Regiments advanced in drizzling rain towards Gheluvelt. Withering fire met them. Ninety minutes later, the assault was over but a few attackers had penetrated the left where a platoon of the 2nd King's Royal Rifle Corps (KRRC) held an orchard just forward of the main defensive line with a company of the 1st Queen's.

The Germans in the orchard began to enfilade the British positions. An immediate counterattack, by a single under-strength KRRC platoon, was unsuccessful. The German artillery saturated the Gheluvelt defences and support zone with high explosive and shrapnel. The 2nd Welch Regiment, astride the road, took heavy casualties. The company south of the road, and on the left of the Queen's, quickly lost 56 men killed and wounded. The CO, Lt.Col. Morland, decided to retire them to the support line until the shelling stopped. A runner, sent to the Queen's with the message of withdrawal, never reached them. They held position, not knowing their flank was now exposed.

North of the road, two companies of the Welch remained next to the South Wales Borderers. Communications to the rear no longer existed. Shrapnel cut down every runner and the telephone wires were destroyed. It was impossible to call up artillery support as the German attacks reached a climax.

At 1000 hours, four battalions from the 54th Reserve Division north of the road, three battalions of the 30th Division south of the road and a further three from the same division in echelon to the rear and left,

This is claimed to be a rare and genuine 1914 photograph showing British troops advancing across open country in the vicinity of Ypres. It was taken by a soldier using a 'vest-pocket' camera and the troops are only about 50 metres from the camera. Careful study shows what could be a mounted officer on the right of the picture and the smoke screen has clearly only just been laid.

advanced. In support tramped a further three battalions from the 16th Bavarian Reserve Regiment. There was a thousand yard gap in the line, Ypres was just 5 km away, and barely 1,000 men stood between the Germans and their objective.

The mass of field-grey surged forward, the men singing and cheering. South of the road, the German barrage failed to lift as the enemy closed with the 1st Queen's and KRRC. Hit by their own gunners, the German infantry faltered and fell back. North of the road, the 1st South Wales Borderers, 1st Scots Guards and the remaining Welch fought frantically to hold their line. In vain. The attack smashed through.

Some Germans reached Gheluvelt village and enfiladed the defence from both sides of the road. The British position began to collapse. The KRRC lost more than 400 men; the 1st Loyals could muster no more than 160 and the 2nd Royal Scots Fusiliers had well under 100 effectives.

The 143rd Infantry Regiment, supported by field guns, hit the 1st Queen's with a flank attack. The Queen's attempted to fight their way out: only two officers and 12 men succeeded. The rest were shot down from the front, the side and the rear. The 143rd Infantry Regiment, frustrated and infuriated by their high casualties, stripped their captives, unwounded or not, of uniforms and possessions, and clubbed and bayoneted some of their prisoners.

The German account of this action attributed their heavy losses to the fact that 'over every bush, hedge and fragment of wall floated a film of smoke, betraying a machine gun rattling out bullets'. It was a further tribute to the musketry of the BEF.

On the right of the 1st Queens, 250 men of the 1st Loyal North Lancashire and 120 men from the 2nd Royal Scots Fusiliers held half a mile of front. They were shelled for most of the morning and in the early afternoon the 105th (Saxon) Regiment advanced against them. There was no hope of reinforcement and retreat was out of the question. They fought for two hours, containing the gap in the line, but were eventually swamped. Only a handful of men escaped. The victorious 105th (Saxon) Infantry Regiment behaved with gallant courtesy to the exhausted men

British troops in front-line trenches at Ypres in early December, 1914. Shortly after this photograph was taken, the BEF started its withdrawal from the sector.

THE CHARGE OF THE 2ND WORCESTERS AT GHELUVELT,
31 OCTOBER 1914
After the fall of Gheluvelt to the Germans, the 2nd
Worcesters were ordered to attempt a counterattack.
Approaching the Château over a thousand yards of open
ground they lost over 100 men, but they managed to break
through and charged the panicked novices of the 16th
Bavarian Reserve, the 244th Reserve and the 245th Reserve
with bayonets. The Germans broke and the Worcesters
restored the line.

who finally put their hands in the air. It was behaviour in stark contrast to that of the 143rd Infantry.

Behind the British positions, there was confusion and an obvious feeling of crisis. There was a stream of wounded; men separated from their comrades wandered around trying to rejoin their units. A few heavy howitzers, ammunition exhausted, moved towards Ypres along the Menin Road, tangled with vehicles, wagons, men and supplies. Enemy shells fell steadily.

Into this scene of chaos rode Haig and his staff. He had received news of the fall of Gheluvelt and came to judge the situation for himself. He was, as ever, impeccably turned out and showed no emotion as he surveyed the scene. 'It was like on parade back at Aldershot,' one soldier recalled many years later, 'and I thought if he's not worried, neither am I.' Haig's gesture may have helped restore confidence, but it was of little use as a source of information. One thing was clear. There was very little to stop Fabeck's men marching to Ypres. Something extraordinary was needed.

RESTORING THE LINE

Something extraordinary was about to happen. Brig.Gen. FitzClarence, commanding 1st (Guards) Brigade had heard of the loss of Gheluvelt. Riding forward, he found remnants of the Scots Guards and the South Wales Borderers grimly holding on behind the château.

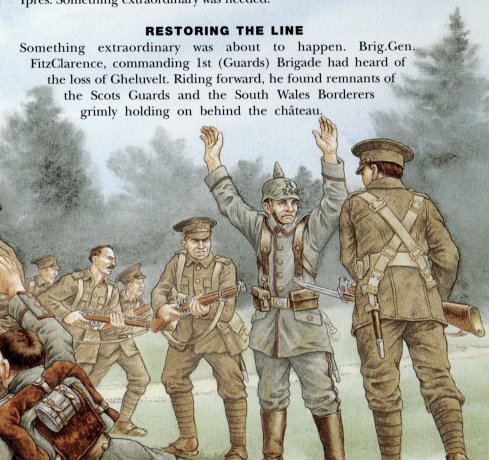

They had a joint headquarters in the stables, but were barely maintaining their position. They expected attacks on both flanks and their rear where the Germans occupied the château itself.

FitzClarence reported to Maj.Gen. Lomax, 1st Division's commander who gave him the last of his reserves, the 2nd Worcesters who were at Polygon Wood. FitzClarence issued a stark command to Maj. Edward Hankey, ordering the battalion, 'to advance without delay and deliver a counterattack with the utmost vigour against the enemy who was in possession of Gheluvelt, and to re-establish our line there.'

While FitzClarence dealt with Hankey, Lomax rode to Hooge Château which housed the commanders and staff of the 1st & 2nd Divisions to discuss defending Ypres itself. As the commanders and their staffs made plans, a German heavy shell crashed into the conference room. Lomax was severely wounded, Monro badly concussed and every officer except one was killed or wounded. It was a fearful blow, but within an hour the command structure was functioning again.

Hankey had three companies, a total of seven officers and 357 men, to use in the attack. He spoke briefly. 'The 2nd Worcesters will take Gheluvelt,' he ordered and paused. 'We can and will do it. Good luck to you all.' The Worcesters moved at 1400 hours. They had eaten a stew,

British troops in the front line at Ypres in late 1914.

received a rum ration, off-loaded their packs and collected extra ammunition. For the first 600 yards, they went in single file until reaching a small belt of trees on the Polderhoek Ridge. There was 1,000 yards of open country between them and the château. The Worcesters halted. Everywhere there were signs of retreat. German shrapnel sprayed the area. Only the Worcesters were going forward.

Hankey spoke quietly to his RSM. 'Are they all up, Sarn't Major?' 'All up, sir!' Hankey deployed his men into two lines. 'Officers to the front! Advance at the double – advance!' he shouted and the 2nd Worcesters pounded across the stubble through increased artillery fire. In the minutes that the Worcesters took to cross the open field, more than 100 men fell. They reached a small wood bordering the château. A brief pause, then rapid clicking as bayonets were fixed before the Worcesters burst out of the trees onto the grass by the château.

About 1,200 soldiers in field-grey were milling around. Some were looting; some searched for water and food; others sniped at the Scots Guards and Borderers on the perimeter, their backs turned to the Worcesters. The sudden eruption of 200 belligerent British soldiers panicked the novices of the 16th Bavarian Reserve Infantry, the 244th Reserve and 245th Reserve. After some brutal bayonet work by the Worcesters, the Germans fled in disorder. Hankey's men reached the remaining Guards and Borderers. The line was restored.

South of the Menin Road, the 105th (Saxon) Regiment failed to exploit its success. The defence line had been peeled open for over a mile. As the Germans moved forward, they took casualties from an *ad hoc* force scraped together by Col. Lovett of the 1st Gloucesters. The Saxons halted. Up came a German field battery, one gun opening fire on the waiting British, 700 yards away. In turn, 54 Battery of the RFA, one of three behind Lovett's men, sent up a single gun with a precious commodity – high explosive shells, the first supplies of which had recently arrived. With its second round, the 54 Battery gun destroyed the German piece. The remaining British guns then fired high explosive and shrapnel and the Germans bolted.

Further south, there was more extremely heavy fighting. The 7th Division, down to 30 per cent of its original strength, and the miscellaneous units under Gen. Bulfin which made up the right wing of the 1st Division, spent a desperate day. The line had nearly collapsed at least three times. Capper of the 7th Division and Bulfin stayed close behind the line, constantly reorganising the defence as casualties mounted. By early afternoon, their men were exhausted but still defiant. Bulfin, with a charming and inspired simplicity, decided that as defence was virtually impossible, the best solution was a counterattack.

With the residue of five battalions, some cavalry, engineers, 'C' Battery of the RHA, the spontaneous help of a company of sappers from 26th Field Company, and the consummate professionals of the 7th Division, Bulfin smashed into his opponents. Astonished, the Germans gave way, albeit reluctantly. Bulfin's action secured the line. His 800 metre-advance was costly: 1,090 officers and men were casualties, but he had secured the position against the enemy's best efforts.

Close by, near Hollebeke and Zandvoorde, the planned French and British offensive ran directly into German infantry waiting to launch their own attack. There was an unexpected bonus. The Allied artillery, well supplied with ammunition for the advance, wreaked havoc among the German troops congregated at their start line. The enemy assault was severely delayed and greatly weakened.

Gracious living. An al fresco break for soldiers of the BEF.

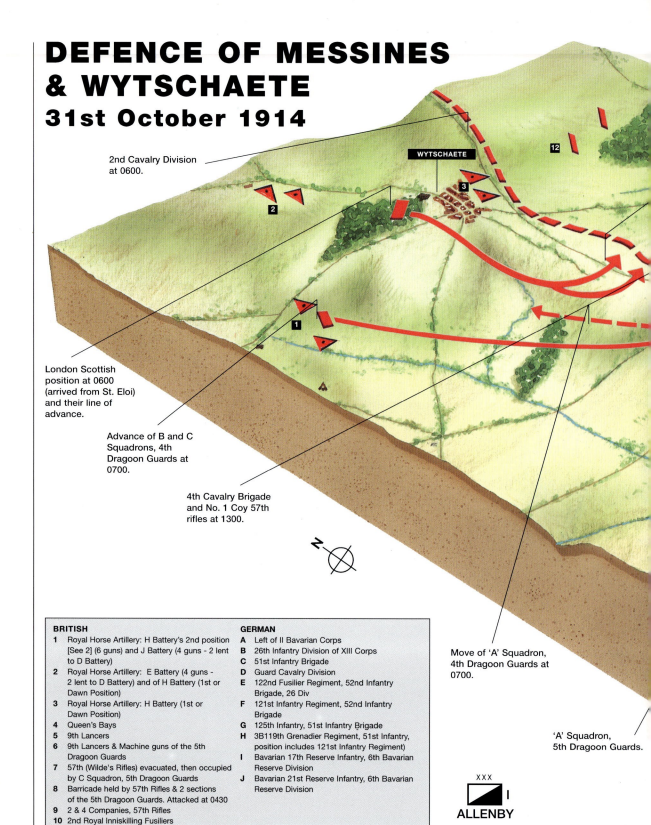

DEFENCE OF MESSINES & WYTSCHAETE
31st October 1914

2nd Cavalry Division at 0600.

WYTSCHAETE

12

2

3

London Scottish position at 0600 (arrived from St. Eloi) and their line of advance.

Advance of B and C Squadrons, 4th Dragoon Guards at 0700.

4th Cavalry Brigade and No. 1 Coy 57th rifles at 1300.

1

N

Move of 'A' Squadron, 4th Dragoon Guards at 0700.

BRITISH

1 Royal Horse Artillery: H Battery's 2nd position [See 2] (6 guns) and J Battery (4 guns - 2 lent to D Battery)
2 Royal Horse Artillery: E Battery (4 guns - 2 lent to D Battery) and of H Battery (1st or Dawn Position)
3 Royal Horse Artillery: H Battery (1st or Dawn Position)
4 Queen's Bays
5 9th Lancers
6 9th Lancers & Machine guns of the 5th Dragoon Guards
7 57th (Wilde's Rifles) evacuated, then occupied by C Squadron, 5th Dragoon Guards
8 Barricade held by 57th Rifles & 2 sections of the 5th Dragoon Guards. Attacked at 0430
9 2 & 4 Companies, 57th Rifles
10 2nd Royal Inniskilling Fusiliers
11 4 Squadron, 5th Dragoon Guards (Relieved by R Inniskilling at about 0300)
12 No 3 Company, 57th Rifles

GERMAN

A Left of II Bavarian Corps
B 26th Infantry Division of XIII Corps
C 51st Infantry Brigade
D Guard Cavalry Division
E 122nd Fusilier Regiment, 52nd Infantry Brigade, 26 Div
F 121st Infantry Regiment, 52nd Infantry Brigade
G 125th Infantry, 51st Infantry Brigade
H 3B119th Grenadier Regiment, 51st Infantry, position includes 121st Infantry Regiment)
I Bavarian 17th Reserve Infantry, 6th Bavarian Reserve Division
J Bavarian 21st Reserve Infantry, 6th Bavarian Reserve Division

'A' Squadron, 5th Dragoon Guards.

XXX
I
ALLENBY

78

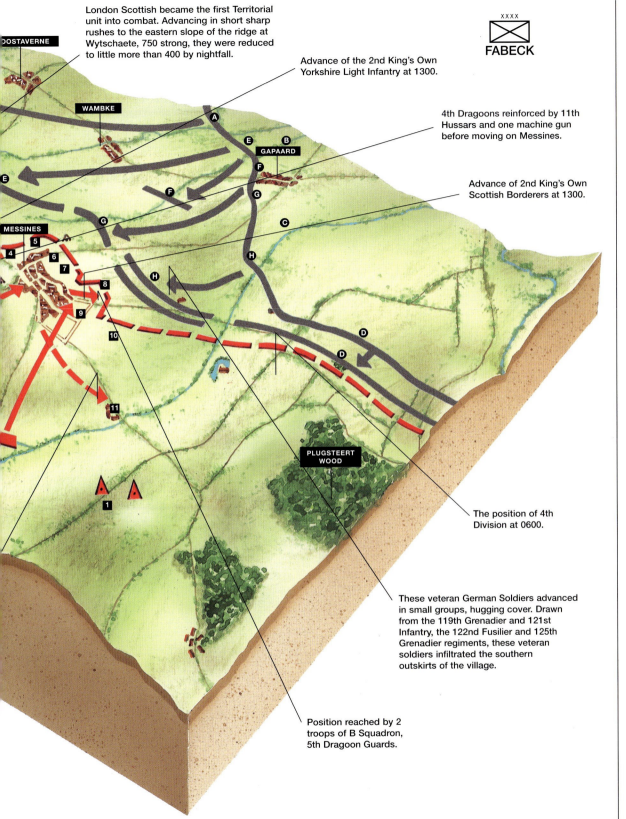

London Scottish became the first Territorial unit into combat. Advancing in short sharp rushes to the eastern slope of the ridge at Wytschaete, 750 strong, they were reduced to little more than 400 by nightfall.

OOSTAVERNE

WAMBKE

Advance of the 2nd King's Own Yorkshire Light Infantry at 1300.

XXXX

FABECK

4th Dragoons reinforced by 11th Hussars and one machine gun before moving on Messines.

GAPAARD

Advance of 2nd King's Own Scottish Borderers at 1300.

MESSINES

PLUGSTEERT WOOD

The position of 4th Division at 0600.

These veteran German Soldiers advanced in small groups, hugging cover. Drawn from the 119th Grenadier and 121st Infantry, the 122nd Fusilier and 125th Grenadier regiments, these veteran soldiers infiltrated the southern outskirts of the village.

Position reached by 2 troops of B Squadron, 5th Dragoon Guards.

A 60-pdr. howitzer in action at Ypres. This photograph is interesting because it clearly shows the early use of camouflage to deter detection from air observation. A network of foliage has been constructed above the gun to mislead enemy airmen – a similar screen may be seen in the photograph of the 18-pdr. at Ypres. The rapid development of accurate artillery observation from the air caused many soldiers, on both sides, to suspect spies were at work, and there is no doubt that innocent French and Belgian civilians were shot as enemy agents by all parties. Claims that the sails of windmills were used to transmit coded messages, that corn was stacked in elaborate patterns to indicate gun positions and that parish priests were seen to be wearing enemy army boots under their cassocks were just three of the rumours which sprang up and were fervently believed.

So much for Gheluvelt. Fabeck's other massive strike was against Messines and the ridge.

MESSINES RIDGE

A heavy bombardment prepared the way for the attack on Messines itself, with nine battalions of German infantry waiting patiently behind the shelling. This would not, however, be the usual solid mass of field-grey advancing into solid rifle fire. The men who faced Allenby's Cavalry Corps went forward in small groups, hugging cover. Drawn from the 119th Grenadier and 121st Infantry, the 122nd Fusilier and 125th Grenadier regiments, these veteran soldiers infiltrated the southern out-skirts of the village. Some 1,000 troopers fought resolutely against six times their number to hold on to the battered ruins and heaps of bricks which had once been homes.

German attacks were pressed all along the Messines-Wytschaete ridge, and facing them, the London Scottish, who became the first Territorial infantry unit to go into action. Advancing in short sharp rushes to the eastern slope of the ridge at Wytschaete, 750 strong, they were reduced to little more than 400 at nightfall.

The action continued for four days; the ridge was lost, regained, lost again in a bitter and chaotic battle. Unlike the fighting at Gheluvelt, the struggle for the Messines Ridge is not easily reduced to descriptions of the action hour by hour. Wytschaete was taken by the enemy, recaptured, lost once more. By 2 November, Fabeck held the ridge, but still faced an unbroken Allied line. The French 32nd Division had been sent by Foch to bolster the defence and the Germans remained a long way from Kemmel.

Haig fully anticipated that 1 November would see a renewed, massive attack along the Menin Road towards Ypres. Increasing pressure at

Messines and military common-sense dictated that a new defensive position was needed to protect Ypres. Unbroken, the British line retreated carefully, abandoning Gheluvelt to the enemy. Although heavy shelling continued, the Germans made only one major infantry assault. Mounted by the 39th Division and brigades of the 4th Bavarian and 30th Divisions, it fell, once more, on the 7th Division and the composite battalions commanded by Gen. Bulfin. There were anxious moments, but the line held.

The BEF was desperately short of men. Of 84 British battalions, only nine had between 300–450 men; 26 mustered 200–300 effectives; 31 were very weak with 100–200 men and 18 had fewer than 100 of all ranks. Some battalions had received no less than six drafts of reinforcements since August.

The attacks continued throughout 2 November. Somehow, the defence line from St Eloi to the Menin Road remained intact. The 30th Division managed to reach Veldhoek, but the French and British held on doggedly. The fighting had lost the horrifying intensity of the first attacks as the Germans became more wary, but the conflict continued its toll.

On the evening of 2 November, Falkenhayn reviewed his options. He did not know if the enemy was really as weak as interrogation of prisoners suggested. Substantial Allied reinforcements might be on the way. He himself could draw more troops from France for another assault in Flanders, or perhaps attack elsewhere. Falkenhayn decided to make one last mighty effort to crumble the Allied defences and take the Channel ports. For the next three days, there was less action at the front. The artillery fell silent for long periods. On 5 November, the 7th Division and the 3rd Infantry Brigade were relieved.

THE FINAL ASSAULT ON YPRES

Falkenhayn ordered supplies to be husbanded for the great attack planned for 10 November. A new Army Group, Linsingen, was created to spearhead this push forward. Linsingen, who commanded II Corps, part of Rupprecht's Sixth Army, was a thrusting officer, with a reputation as a man who got things done. His new Army Group consisted of XV Corps from Army Group Fabeck, made up of the 30th and 39th Divisions, the 4th division whose Pomeranians and West Prussians were considered to be the finest troops in the German Army, and the Kaiser's beloved Guards. The 1st and 3rd Foot Guards and the 2nd and 4th Guard Grenadier regiments.

The attack would be launched from Polygon Wood to north of the Menin Road; von Fabeck's remaining troops would both press forward on the southern flank and support Army Group Linsingen by enfilade fire. The Sixth Army, at La Bassée and Armentières, and the Fourth Army which held the front north of Ypres to the coast, were to attack energetically to prevent the Allies moving reserves from one sector to another. The 4th Division and the

This photograph of British infantry 'in the firing line' is typical of a number which appeared at the time. The location is 'somewhere near Ypres'. Undoubtedly taken when there were no enemy troops in the immediate vicinity, and showing an impressive number of men to the yard, it nonetheless shows well the primitive and cramped conditions.

THE ASSAULT OF THE PRUSSIAN GUARD, YPRES
11th November 1914

XXX
HAIG

The infantry assault began at 0900 hours after 2 hours of artillery bombardment. The 1st & 3rd Foot Guards were ordered to advance north-westwards, the dividing line between the regiments being the south west corner of Nonneboschen. The 2nd & 4th Guard Grenadier Regiments were to advance due west - in other words, on a diverging course. It was planned to insert Battalion II of the 2nd Guard Grenadiers from the Brigade Reserve into the gap but this move was prevented by the British artillery.

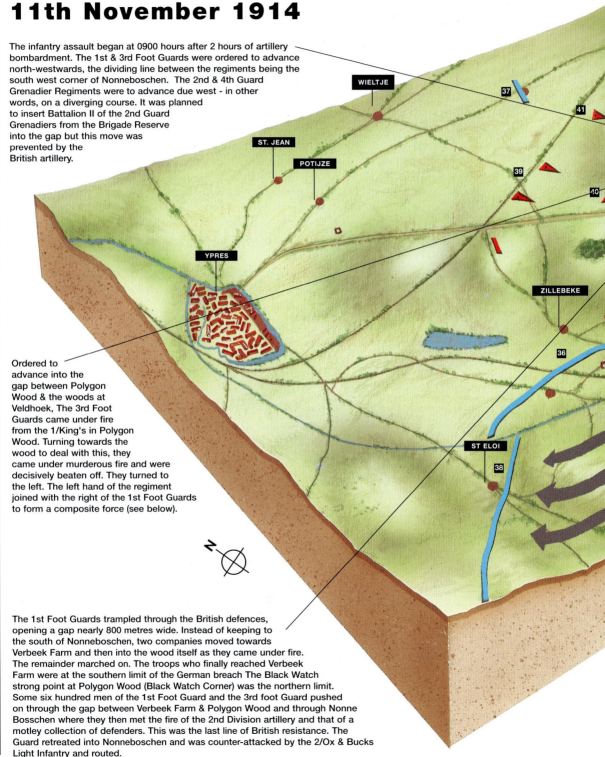

WIELTJE

37

41

ST. JEAN

POTIJZE

39

40

YPRES

ZILLEBEKE

3

36

Ordered to advance into the gap between Polygon Wood & the woods at Veldhoek, The 3rd Foot Guards came under fire from the 1/King's in Polygon Wood. Turning towards the wood to deal with this, they came under murderous fire and were decisively beaten off. They turned to the left. The left hand of the regiment joined with the right of the 1st Foot Guards to form a composite force (see below).

ST ELOI

38

The 1st Foot Guards trampled through the British defences, opening a gap nearly 800 metres wide. Instead of keeping to the south of Nonneboschen, two companies moved towards Verbeek Farm and then into the wood itself as they came under fire. The remainder marched on. The troops who finally reached Verbeek Farm were at the southern limit of the German breach The Black Watch strong point at Polygon Wood (Black Watch Corner) was the northern limit. Some six hundred men of the 1st Foot Guard and the 3rd foot Guard pushed on through the gap between Verbeek Farm & Polygon Wood and through Nonne Bosschen where they then met the fire of the 2nd Division artillery and that of a motley collection of defenders. This was the last line of British resistance. The Guard retreated into Nonneboschen and was counter-attacked by the 2/Ox & Bucks Light Infantry and routed.

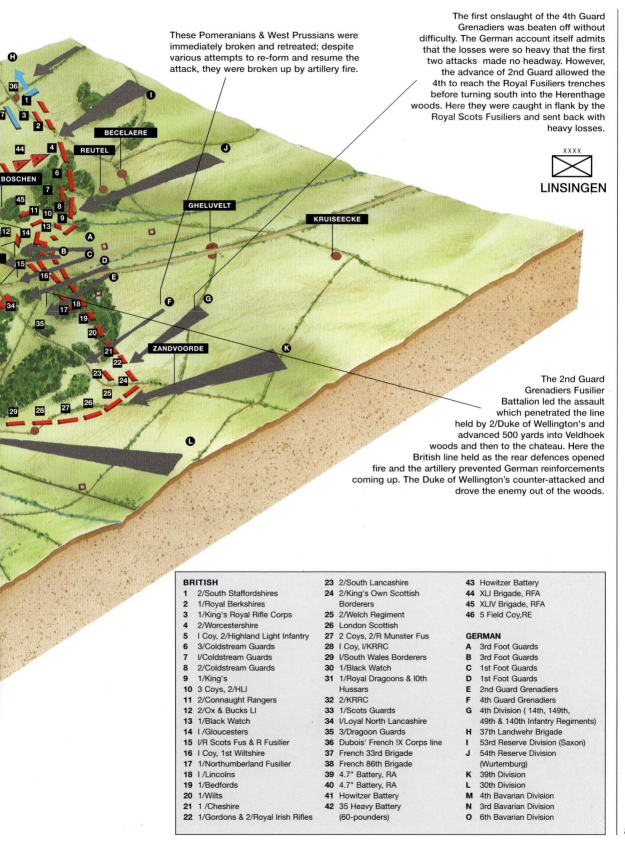

These Pomeranians & West Prussians were immediately broken and retreated; despite various attempts to re-form and resume the attack, they were broken up by artillery fire.

The first onslaught of the 4th Guard Grenadiers was beaten off without difficulty. The German account itself admits that the losses were so heavy that the first two attacks made no headway. However, the advance of 2nd Guard allowed the 4th to reach the Royal Fusiliers trenches before turning south into the Herenthage woods. Here they were caught in flank by the Royal Scots Fusiliers and sent back with heavy losses.

XXXX

LINSINGEN

The 2nd Guard Grenadiers Fusilier Battalion led the assault which penetrated the line held by 2/Duke of Wellington's and advanced 500 yards into Veldhoek woods and then to the chateau. Here the British line held as the rear defences opened fire and the artillery prevented German reinforcements coming up. The Duke of Wellington's counter-attacked and drove the enemy out of the woods.

BECELAERE
REUTEL
BOSCHEN
GHELUVELT
KRUISEECKE
ZANDVOORDE

BRITISH		
1	2/South Staffordshires	
2	1/Royal Berkshires	
3	1/King's Royal Rifle Corps	
4	2/Worcestershire	
5	I Coy, 2/Highland Light Infantry	
6	3/Coldstream Guards	
7	I/Coldstream Guards	
8	2/Coldstream Guards	
9	1/King's	
10	3 Coys, 2/HLI	
11	2/Connaught Rangers	
12	2/Ox & Bucks LI	
13	1/Black Watch	
14	I /Gloucesters	
15	I/R Scots Fus & R Fusilier	
16	I Coy, 1st Wiltshire	
17	1/Northumberland Fusilier	
18	I /Lincolns	
19	1/Bedfords	
20	1/Wilts	
21	1 /Cheshire	
22	1/Gordons & 2/Royal Irish Rifles	

23	2/South Lancashire
24	2/King's Own Scottish Borderers
25	2/Welch Regiment
26	London Scottish
27	2 Coys, 2/R Munster Fus
28	I Coy, I/KRRC
29	I/South Wales Borderers
30	1/Black Watch
31	1/Royal Dragoons & I0th Hussars
32	2/KRRC
33	1/Scots Guards
34	I/Loyal North Lancashire
35	3/Dragoon Guards
36	Dubois' French !X Corps line
37	French 33rd Brigade
38	French 86th Brigade
39	4.7" Battery, RA
40	4.7" Battery, RA
41	Howitzer Battery
42	35 Heavy Battery (60-pounders)

43	Howitzer Battery
44	XLI Brigade, RFA
45	XLIV Brigade, RFA
46	5 Field Coy,RE

GERMAN	
A	3rd Foot Guards
B	3rd Foot Guards
C	1st Foot Guards
D	1st Foot Guards
E	2nd Guard Grenadiers
F	4th Guard Grenadiers
G	4th Division (14th, 149th, 49th & 140th Infantry Regiments)
H	37th Landwehr Brigade
I	53rd Reserve Division (Saxon)
J	54th Reserve Division (Wurtemburg)
K	39th Division
L	30th Division
M	4th Bavarian Division
N	3rd Bavarian Division
O	6th Bavarian Division

Guards would advance each side of the Menin Road. From Polygon Wood to Messines, 12 German divisions would crash against a desperately thin Allied line.

It rained. There was persistent fog. The roads, muddy and narrow, needed reinforcing before the heavy guns could be moved into position, and the fog prevented reconnaissance. A 24 hour delay was agreed. Thus, the final assault on Ypres, designed to finish the war, began at dawn on 11 November, a day which would eventually be remembered for other reasons.

A massive bombardment began promptly at 0630 hours. The shelling was fiercest where newly-arrived units of II Corps had taken over the line from the 7th Division. As 0900 approached, the shells began to move towards the British rear zones. The infantry attack would soon follow.

On the right and the left of the Allied lines, the Germans showed little inclination to press home the assault. These were men who had faced the enemy many times in the previous days and lacked enthusiasm for the task in hand. At Messines, the attack was so feeble that Allenby was able to detach troops to reinforce the British line at the centre, against the German Guard and 4th Division.

They came out of the mist, 17,500 men, ranks dressed, the officers with drawn swords. The 4th Division was immediately broken by the rhythmic fire of II Corps. It was Mons and Le Cateau all over again. Lashed by shrapnel and high explosive, whipped by small arms fire, the élite Prussians and Pomeranians fell back. They mounted another attack late in the afternoon which also collapsed. The men of II Corps hardly considered themselves to have been troubled.

It was down to the Guard. Four regiments, each of three battalions, each battalion in column, marched towards Ypres. To the immediate south of the road, the 4th Guard Grenadiers went steadfastly forward, in

The repulse of the Prussian Guard Divisions on 11 November, 1914 effectively marked the end of von Falkenhayn's attempts to capture Calais. The British press of the time seized upon the action and turned it into a defeat of monumental proportions. The Guard was elevated into near-mythical status, and one paper even went so far as to allege that the Kaiser broke down and wept when he learned the news. There is no doubt that the Guard, like all picked household troops, were formidable opponents who fought with considerable courage. Here, Kaiser Wilhelm II takes the salute in pre-war Berlin.

disciplined and apparently indestructible ranks into a hail of rifle fire. They took frightening losses, officers and men dropping with fearful regularity.

A British artillery officer in a forward observation post, whose telephone line had been cut, sprinted back to his battery as the German Guard approached. The gunners loaded shrapnel and the 4th Guard Grenadiers shivered, reeled and broke.

Astride and north of the road, the 2nd Guard Grenadiers found a gap between a company of the French 4th Zouaves and the 4th Royal Fusiliers. The Fusiliers had wisely retired to their support line during the shelling and doubled forward as it lifted. But the Guard were swift and the British were surprised, being forced back with the Zouaves into Herenthage woods.

The 2nd Guard Grenadiers made the first breach in the British line, their leading battalion following the defenders into the wood. They were unsupported on their flanks, however. The thick undergrowth disguised a counterattack by the 1st Royal Scots Fusiliers and 2nd Royal Sussex on their left. Another on the right by the 2nd Duke of Wellington's pushed them back to the former British firing line. Here they held and a dangerous bulge was created in the Allied line. To the north, a much wider hole was made.

Brig.Gen. FitzClarence, who had been so instrumental in recovering Gheluvelt, and his 1st (Guards) Brigade faced the 1st Foot Guards. Fitz-Clarence only had one unit remaining from his original command, but had acquired two others – the 1st Black Watch and the 1st Cameron Highlanders to go with the 1st Scots Guards. On the right of the German 1st Foot Guards strode the 3rd Foot Guards, and the six battalions rolled over their opponents in minutes aiming for the gap between Veldhoek and Polygon Wood.

The huge consumption of material in a modern war caught the British – and the other combatants – unprepared. The War Office had assumed that the BEF would fight four great battles in the first two months of the war and that each would last for three days and the supplies and organisation of the BEF were made in accordance with this scale. Government policy encouraged the belief that no more than six divisions would fight in a European war which would last only three months. In this picture, the SS Moorgate is discharging her cargo in a seemingly leisurely fashion.

Men on the right of the German Guard dropped as they came under fire from the 1st King's who occupied Polygon Wood. The 54th Reserve Division had been detailed to attack the wood that morning, but had shown no stomach for the task. The 3rd wheeled towards the wood. The 1st King's began to fire in earnest. The 1st continued onwards, suddenly finding themselves checked by a handful of Black Watch and Scots Guards. Before they could eliminate this nuisance, British artillery began to lob shrapnel into the ranks of the leading battalion and the 1st Foot Guard lost its cohesion. Many of them ran for the Nonnebosschen (Nun's Wood) which lay between Polygon Wood and the Menin Road.

From Polygon Wood itself, the men of the 1st King's kept their eye on what seemed to be another assault by the 3rd Foot Guard. Minutes passed and the field grey line stayed motionless. The smoke and fog cleared in a freshening wind and the King's realised that the attack line was, in fact, heaped enemy dead.

THE BATTLE OF NONNEBOSCHEN

The 1st Foot Guard had almost 900 men in Nonnebosschen, but they had lost many of their officers and senior NCOs. Maj.Gen. Landon, commanding the 1st Division, ordered the 2nd Ox & Bucks Light Infantry to clear the wood of the enemy. They moved up to the wood at 1400 hours and 'A' and 'B' Companies charged into the wood in open order. A company from the Northamptons joined them, as did the 5th Field Company of the Royal Engineers who rushed forward when they saw the attack go in.

The Guard was unnerved and ran from the wood – like pheasants, thought one British observer – first an odd one or two, then small groups of two or three, and then a rush. Those who did not surrender met determined rifle fire.

Some 600 Germans of the 1st Foot Guard and 3rd Foot Guard had managed to pass the strong point manned by the Black Watch and had marched on, Nonnebosschen on their right, to within sight of part of the line of the 2nd Divisional artillery. The gunners opened fire and the Guard scattered. Most turned and ran, but a few sought cover in some cottages close to Nonnebosschen. Two well-aimed shells destroyed one house. The other was stormed by five pugnacious cooks and duty men of the 5th Field Company, Royal Engineers.

The last German guardsmen fled, unaware that they had reached the last British defences before the Channel coast.

So ended First Ypres. Fighting, sometimes fierce, continued for a few more days, but Falkenhayn decided to cut his losses. On 17 November, he decided to abandon the offensive. Between 15 and 22 November, the relief and reorganisation of the British line took place. Foch's troops took over the Ypres salient and the British established a front of 21 miles from Givenchy to Kemmel. The casualties at Ypres, the recital of losses, the repetition of figures, numbs the mind. It is enough that the 7th Division, in one month from 7 October to the 5 November lost just over 10,000 all ranks from its initial strength of more than 12,000. I Corps lost over half its effectives. British official figures give a total, including the Indian Corps, of 58,155 all ranks killed, wounded and missing from 14 October to 30 November. The old British Regular Army was effectively destroyed.

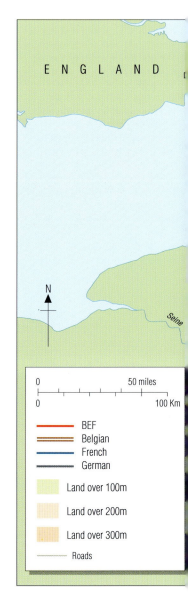

ENGLAND

N

Seine

0					50 miles
0					100 Km

— BEF
— Belgian
— French
— German

Land over 100m

Land over 200m

Land over 300m

— Roads

German casualty figures cannot be ascertained with accuracy. Their recording system was different and, according to one source, there were not enough clerks to make the records – 'casualty reports ... were returned only very irregularly ... and losses are impossible of compilation'. It is certain that they were very high indeed – not for nothing did the Germans refer to the battles around Ypres in the autumn of 1914 as *Der Kindermord bei Ypern* – the Massacre of the Innocents at Ypres – because of the carnage among the youthful volunteers. Official German records admit losses of 134,315 for the period 15 October to the 24 November. Subsequent research suggests that they were double this amount.

On 22 November, the British Army had a quiet day. In London, an administrative procedure was completed. Britain officially declared war against Germany.

THE WESTERN FRONT 15 NOVEMBER 1914

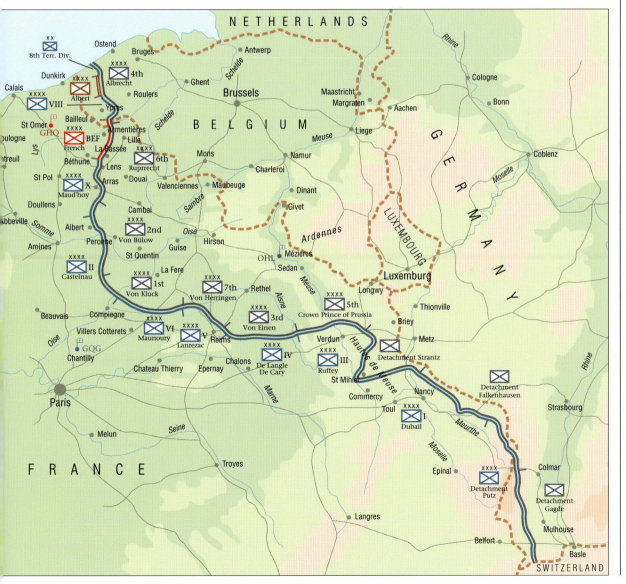

THE BATTLEFIELD TODAY

The fighting areas of late 1914 were to see much more blood in the years that followed. For the student of the Battles of Second and Third Ypres, the modern scenery bears little resemblance to that of 1915 or 1917. Today though, the area would be familiar to the soldiers of the old British Expeditionary Force.

After the war had ended, the Belgian authorities decided that everything would be restored to its 1914 appearance. Roads were reconstructed on their former routes; streams and dykes, rivers and ditches followed their old courses. Most important of all, public buildings were built as copies of their former selves. Today, it is possible to see the countryside in much the same way as those original soldiers of 1914 saw it. There are, of course, differences. Development cannot be stopped and new houses straggle over parts of the battlefield. Children play in a recreation ground close to a housing estate on the Messiness Ridge. Not far from where they practise basketball, the London Scottish charged. In the vicinity of a car showroom, men of the 7th Division dug in and grimly waited for another attack. Even so, it takes just a little imagination to imagine how it was.

For the enthusiast exploring the story of the Battle of First Ypres, the battle which held the Channel Ports, there is much to be seen, especially if one is ready to leave the motor car behind and go on foot or by bicycle. A bicycle is perhaps the best way to appreciate the ground – going up the Messines Ridge in a headwind convinces even the most sceptical of the importance of high ground.

Part of the Messines Ridge today; the four subsequent years of war destroyed much of the area, but the countryside is now very similar in appearance to how it looked when the BEF arrived in October 1914. Although modern developments have begun to erode the battlefield, a map and an eye for detail can still discern the fighting area with little difficulty.

WARGAMING THE YPRES CAMPAIGN

The first battle of Ypres offers enormous scope for wargaming, whether you prefer board-games or figure-games. It is obviously an excellent subject for a 'megagame' with teams of players for each headquarters, each able to see only their immediate area — and hapless commanders-in-chief making the best they can of fragmentary reports which have usually been overtaken by events by the time they arrive. However, since most of us are lucky to have half-a-dozen players available, let alone the fifty or so demanded for a true megagame, I will concentrate on the sort of wargames feasible at ordinary club level.

To simulate the battle of Ypres, whether you cover the crises of 22–3 October or 10–11 November or attempt the whole campaign is going to require a boardgame-style treatment. I say 'boardgame style', because some recent 'operational level' wargames rules are using figures/micro-tanks as counters to move across the map rather like the troop blocks in *kriegspiel* games. This is not just prettier than die-cut cardboard counters, but easier for those of us who have never really learned the NATO-standard military unit symbols generally used in boardgames – and which feel inappropriate to World War I anyway.

Since the BEF ended up in a salient 15 miles across (with an actual frontage of 20–25 miles) a 1/50,000 or even 1/100,000 map is required as a basis to work with. To regulate movement over the map it is generally easier to divide it into areas, or impose a hexagonal grid over the map and use a traditional boardgame style movement system. Area movement demands careful thought: you need to allow the same options available

While the professional British army died at Ypres, recruiting was in full swing in Britain. This rare 1914 picture shows some of the men enlisting in Cardiff. The sergeant appears to be an artilleryman, but the cap badges of the other two men in uniform cannot be clearly distinguished. There are few photographs of black soldiers in the British Army itself during the First World War and this picture is thus of considerable interest.

STORMING NONNEBOSCHEN
Having been broken by murderous fire, around 900 men of the German 1st Foot Guards ran into Nonneboschen (Nun's wood). The 2nd Ox and Bucks Light Infantry were given the task of clearing them out. At 1400 hours 'A' and 'B' Companies charged into the wood in open order. The Guard was unnerved and fled the wood, those who didn't surrender were met with determined rifle fire.

to the historical commanders, so deciding the size and boundaries of each area can take some time. On the other hand, it is an interesting exercise in itself, and area movement makes for simpler rules, easier to remember. The traditional hex movement system demands less initial effort, although deciding how big the hex grid should be poses similar questions. A British brigade or German regiment is the smallest formation a game on the whole battle should be dealing with. Since these occupied a maximum frontage of about 2 miles, that seems a sensible size for each hex, giving, for example, a map 48 hexes across from the forest of Houthurst to Armentières.

A two-mile hex also gives sensible ranges: small arms fire can be exchanged between hexes, with field artillery able to engage up to 2 hexes, and corps level heavy guns up to 3 or 4 if observation could be organised. Long range artillery fire will be of small value in the woods or towns, where targets are hard to locate, but anyone defending the Messines ridge against an enemy approaching from the east can be pounded by every gun in range: as happened to the British cavalry division in the historical battle. A two-mile hex also makes movement rules easy: this is the distance unencumbered infantry were expected the travel over good ground in one hour. However, delays in the dissemination of orders and the confusion prevailing at most headquarters often reduced the theoretical daily march rates. And once in close contact with the enemy, movement — whether forward or backward — was drastically slowed.

That ancient rules device the 'zone of control' is actually rather useful in an Ypres game. Mounted reconnaissance was difficult to press home in the face of quick-fire artillery and magazine-loading rifles. So cavalry must risk losses and enter the ZOC to discover what lurks in the adjacent hex, otherwise the enemy remain unknown and are still free to manoeuvre. As we have seen, both sides began the campaign in ignorance of enemy strengths and intentions. An 'open game' in which all forces are visible to the enemy is clearly unsuitable: counters must be inverted or strengths otherwise concealed or the British will dig in immediately instead of attacking and the Germans' newly-created 4th Army will be detected immediately it enters the map.

Another hallowed concept of boardgame design is the rule of thumb whereby a 3:1 superiority is regarded as the threshold required for a successful attack (where there are no significant terrain or other variables affecting the result). Yet German assaults often enjoyed more than twice that ratio of rifles and guns to the British, and were still beaten off. So you must adjust your combat results table to reflect the superior marksmanship and gunnery of the BEF compared to the often primitive tactics adopted by the Germans. Sir Douglas Haig's diary entry for 24 October 1914 was typical: 'the enemy came on five times in columns of fours. The Oxford and Bucks [Light Infantry] waited to fire until the enemy arrived within fifty yards, and then simply mowed them down.'

Even when the Germans did mass enough men and guns to capture a position, they were frequently ejected from it by a prompt counter-attack. Whatever combat system you adopt, even a successful attack should leave the victors in a state of considerable disorder and vulnerable to a counter-stroke even from a comparatively small force. One major reason for the British success identified by the official historians was the skill of brigade and divisional commanders at mounting counter-attacks at very short notice, often with reserves quietly assembled from sections of the line not under immediate threat. Tension should rise as the game progresses and the British run out of reserves with which to counter-attack. Historically, the British line was stretched to breaking point, prompting Sir John French's celebrated remark to Foch: 'I have no men left but the sentries at my gate. I will take them with me to where the line is broken, and the last of the English will be killed fighting.'

Movement, combat and supply rules can be as complex as you desire, but since one of the key features of the historical campaign was the lack of reliable intelligence, I would favour keeping them as simple as possible. Some sort of hidden movement system is essential: be in face-down counters (with blanks for added fun) or Columbia-style wooden blocks which disguise the strength and identity of your units from the enemy. In 1914, British understanding of the German army was actually very good, due in no small part to the efforts of General Grierson whose tragic death en route for the front catapulted Smith-Dorrien into command of II Corps. However, no-one had anticipated the Germans' immediate use of all their reserve troops, nor had the British or French any inkling that the Germans were recruiting new divisions of volunteers. The XXII, XXIII, XXVI and XXVII Reserve Corps suddenly appeared south of Bruges in mid-October just when Sir John French thought he could resume the offensive. Subsequent German reinforcements came as an equally disagreeable surprise. As Haig lamented, only after the event were the attackers were identified as the Prussian Guard, 'an entirely new body of troops which had been able to concentrate in this area without any information of the movement being received by the Allied Forces.'

German intelligence on the French army was very good, but villainously poor regarding the British army, which was the responsibility of a section tasked with studying many other countries. Few German officers were familiar with the organisation of the British army which was very different to prevailing structures in all other European

'Will They Never Come?' This picture appeared, coincidentally, on the day on which the First Battle of Ypres was later officially deemed to have ended – 22 November 1914, the last day on which it was possible to qualify for the bar to the 1914 Star and to enjoy, in later years, the title of 'Old Contemptible'.

Following on from the example set by Queen Victoria in the South African War, the King and Queen and other members of the Royal Family arranged for Christmas gifts to be sent to the soldiers serving at the front. These were mainly tins containing cigarettes, tobacco and chocolate, but there were also sets of writing paper and other useful items. On the other side of the lines, the Kaiser, the Crown Prince and the King of Bavaria and other rulers made a similar gesture. Many of the gifts were not used but sent home by the recipients as souvenirs. This picture shows soldiers signing for Princess Mary's Gift.

forces. For instance, a German artillery brigade had 72 guns; a British field artillery brigade had just 18; German infantry brigades consisted of two regiments each of six battalions, while British brigades had four single-battalion regiments. Small wonder that German intelligence repeatedly overestimated British strength. As Brigadier Edmonds, the British official historian observed, 'To a German therefore, an infantry brigade meant six battalions, not four, and if a prisoner said he belonged to the blankshire regiment, the German might possibly believe he had identified three battalions.' The German wartime account of Ypres (published in 1917 while the awful Third Battle of Ypres was taking place) betrays this very ignorance, describing the 1/King's (Liverpool) Regiment as the *Konigsregiment Liverpool* and presenting its struggle with the Prussian *Garde Regiment zu fuss* as '*garde gegen garde*' ('guard against guard') as if the three battalion-strong Prussian Guard regiment was the same size as the considerably diminished single battalion of the King's. It is perhaps because of these mistakes that the German account of Ypres repeatedly claims that the British were receiving reinforcements. In an Ypres wargame, the German player(s) should be left as puzzled as their historical counterparts whose every intelligence summary predicted the exhaustion of the enemy reserves. (A feature that would be encountered again and again – and on both sides – during subsequent battles on the western front.)

If you would prefer to concentrate on minor tactics: the manoeuvring of companies and battalions rather than something as daunting as Army Group Fabeck, the Ypres campaign includes some of the most celebrated actions of the war. The most famous is probably the 2/Worcesters' counter-attack at Ghelvelt which was often described as the attack 'that saved the Empire'. However, the assault of the Prussian Guard on 11 November or the struggle for Bixschoote all lend themselves to tactical games with counters or figures.

There was a lively debate before 1914 on the wisdom of night attacks. The Boer War and Russo-Japanese war had revealed the ability of magazine-loading rifles to stop even the most determined attack, provided the defenders kept their nerves. All armies trained their men to attack with the utmost vigour, which is why the French and Austrian armies lost more than half their regular officers in the summer of 1914. As we have seen, British and German officer casualties were almost as severe. Attacking under cover of darkness deprived the defence of its best weapons, the long range firepower of both rifles and quick-fire guns. Covered artillery batteries were unable to bring down observed fire. Yet, as pre-war discussions had emphasised, the attackers were bound to lose cohesion and they could not co-ordinate their artillery fire either.

There were many night attacks during the Ypres campaign, all armies accepting the inevitable confusion as an acceptable price to pay for avoiding the casualties associated with a daylight assault. The Belgian army, not often singled out for praise by British historians actually made numerous night counter-attacks, recapturing villages lost during the day. The cover of darkness was, of course, no guarantee of victory. In *Fifteen Rounds a Minute*, Major 'Ma' Jeffreys, 2/Grenadier Guards, describes yet another counter-attack led by the redoubtable Brigadier-General Fitzclarence. Against an enemy of unknown strength, across ground known only to the commander, and undertaken by exhausted companies that had suffered terrible losses, it was only countermanded when Fitzclarence was shot dead at the head of the column. Other equally foolhardy affairs were launched. and failed with heavy losses.

The Germans were not immune to the chaos attending night attacks. The 17th Reserve Infantry Regiment captured Wytschaete during the night, only to be driven out of it the following morning by a ferocious German artillery bombardment. Wearing the *feldmutze* rather than the *picklehaube*, the unfortunate Bavarians were then shot down by the 21st Reserve Infantry Regiment when they withdrew.

Night attacks are probably best wargamed with the player(s) on one side and an umpire managing the opposition. The possibilities for confusion can only really be exploited with four or more players all on the

The military on all sides were swift to embrace the new technology of wireless signalling. Often accused of a lack of innovative thought, commanders on all sides were often indecently ready to accept fresh ideas and new technology. Communications were always a cause dear to a general's heart. The use of semaphore by flags or heliograph had clear limitations, not least being the need to be able to see the signal source. Wireless overcame that problem, and armies developed specialist skills and equipment – the signals cart had a generator and aerial which could rapidly be assembled and put to work. Other problems were to result; from the very first weeks of the war, all sides were intercepting each other's wireless messages and the use of codes was quickly introduced to prevent this. It was another facet of industrial warfare which is often overlooked.

same side. Communications are unreliable, with messages arriving late or not at all. The players are kept apart, firstly to help the umpire enforce the communications restrictions, and secondly to simulate the terrible isolation experienced by junior officers having to make momentous decisions on their own. It cannot be emphasised too often that wargames are usually better if the rules for movement and combat are ruthlessly simplified. This enables you to run fast-paced games with well-structured communications rules creating the sort of 'friction' so conspicuous in the Ypres campaign, yet so often absent from wargames.

To simulate the whole campaign requires a map or boardgame; tactical actions work well on map or tabletop, but do not overlook the opportunities for role-playing games if you have sufficient players. The bald statement that 1st Ypres was the death of the old British regular Army is seen so often, it can take a role-play game to hammer home exactly what that meant. At the end of November 1914, the average number of men per battalion who had been in the ranks when it landed in August was just 30! And of the officers in a typical battalion, only a single one was likely to be a survivor of the original expeditionary force. The BEF numbered 84,000 in August 1914. During October and November alone it lost 58,000. Take a group of role-players through the saga of long marches, desperate rearguard actions, more marches, ambushes and more improvised defences until they find themselves clinging to a village outside Ypres that will take the British army three years and hundreds of thousands of casualties to recapture. As 'characters' are killed, captured or evacuated back to England, they are replaced. If the game is suitably plotted, you should end with one (or none) of the originals still in the line at the end of the Ypres campaign. The 'Imperial Police Force', the late Victorian British army so lovingly depicted by Kipling has gone for ever.

Another example of the so-called limited and inhibited military mind. Despite their quaint appearance and, undoubted mechanical unreliability, the armoured car quickly made an appearance. This photograph, taken immediately before the war, shows some early British endeavours. The cyclists acted as scouts, going on ahead to find the enemy. British armoured cars, under naval command, were at Antwerp and dashed around the countryside, shooting at any German cavalry they encountered. One made a brief appearance near Lille, disconcerting British and German alike with bursts of machine gun fire before vanishing as suddenly as it had arrived.

INDEX

(References to illustrations are shown in **bold**.)

3/0